ASPECTS OF GLOBAL ECONOMIC SHIFTS

by
ELIJAH ABUOI AROK

The publisher wishes to acknowledge and thank Dr. Douglas H. Johnson for his invaluable help and support for Africa World Books and its mission of preserving and promoting African cultural and literary traditions and history. Dr. Johnson and fellow historians have been instrumental in ensuring that African people remain connected to their past and their identity. Africa World Books is proud to carry on this mission.

Copyright © 2023 Elijah Abuoi Arok

ISBN: 978-0-6457590-3-7

No part of this publication may be reproduced, stored in a retrieval system, or transmitted, in any form, or by any means, electronic, mechanical, photocopying, recording or otherwise, without the prior permission of the publishers.

This book is sold subject to the conditions that it shall not, by way of trade or otherwise, be lent, re-sold, hired out or otherwise circulated without the publisher's prior consent in any form of binding or cover other than in which it is published and without a similar condition including the condition being imposed on the subsequent purchaser.

Cover design, typesetting and layout: Africa World Books
Unit 3, 57 Frobisher St, Osborne Park, WA 6017
P.O. Box 1106 Osborne Park, WA 6916

CONTENTS

Author Autobiography	v
Abstract	xv
Introduction	1
Africa's First Light Rail System	3
Implications	4
Social Ethics In Civilisation	4
Will Of God	9
Single Parents For Economic Inequality	16
Preventing Alcohol And Substance Abuse With God's Word	19
A World Of Rapid Change	20
Violence In Schools	21
Materialism	22
Obesity	23
Educational Disparity	25
Practice Of Education	29
The Teaching Comes From God	32
Spiritual Erosion of National Pride and Identity	34
Economic Poverty	35

Facing the Growing Unemployment Challenges in Africa	36
Unemployment in the Bible	37
Promises for those Struggling with Unemployment	38
Core Challenges for Northern Africa Include the Following	41
Core Challenges For Sub-Saharan Africa Include The Following	42
Urban Growth and Urbanisation	42
Advantages of Urbanisation	43
Disadvantages of Urbanisation	43
Superstitious Beliefs	51
Gender Discrimination	53
Caste Discrimination	56
Health And Safety	57
Biblical Health Principles	58
Religion In The Bible	60
Jesus Criticizes The Religious Leaders	62
Why Religion (Alone) Can't Save You (John 3:1-7)	65
Does God Oppose Religious Freedom in the Old Testament?	70
How to Believe in God	72
The Globalisation of Culture	72
The Effects of Globalisation in the 21st Century	74
The New World Order	76
The Deadliest Diseases in the World	77
What Does The Bible Say About Pandemic Diseases/Sicknesses?	79
What Does the Bible Say about Coping/Dealing with a Terminal Illness?	81
How Can a Christian Cope While Suffering with a Degenerative Disease?	82
Why Does God Allow Sickness?	84
God Knew us Before we Were Born	86

The People Who Know Their God	87
How Did People Know	90
About God Before the Bible?	90
How Can I Come to Really Know God?	91
The Unknown God in Acts 17:23	93
Living in a World of Lies	96
The Ninth Commandment	100
Conclusion	104
Bibliography	*109*

AUTHOR AUTOBIOGRAPHY

I was born on January 1st, 1968 at Khok in Toch, 50 miles from Adhiok's old home, in Jonglei State, where we lived near the Nile River with my family. As a nomad, access to basic education has long been a challenge for South Sudanese communities, and I was not alone; Southern State was home to over 4,565 911 of the country's out-of-school nomadic children ages 6-11 in 1979. Nationwide, as many children were left out of the education system and more than half of them were girls. Citizens in rural areas, and disadvantaged groups such as nomads and pastoralists, traditionally suffer higher rates of education exclusion.

Parental Careers
It seems like many of us follow in our parents' footsteps when it comes to choosing a career, but in reality, how often does it actually happen? And if we don't follow our parents into the same line of work, how do their occupations affect what we ultimately end up doing ourselves? The result is an interactive visualization that maps father-son occupation pairs and mother-daughter occupation pairs – there's no crossing of the streams, incompetently, so you can't see father-daughter or mother-son. My father's occupation was mapped to major occupation

categories (multiple careers) namely farmer, fisherman, hunter, Cattle keeper and warrior.

The occupation of mother: A housewife (also known as a homemaker or a stay-at-home mother/mum) is a woman whose work is managing her family's home — housekeeping, which includes caring for her children; cleaning and maintaining the home. My mother had been housewife/farmer, a married woman whose main occupation was caring for her family, managing household affairs, and doing housework. Whereas a career comprises the work activities that can be identified with a particular job or profession, having multiple careers is the growing trend in the late 20th century and early 21st century.

Reflections on my Educational Journey
Prior to the Second Sudanese Civil War: In May of 1979-83, I went to Werkak/ Pabarcikok Elementary schools, the former educational ladder 6 + 3 + 3 was changed in 1990. The primary language at all levels was Arabic, whereas the south has its own diverse, mostly non-Arabic languages and cultures. It was with few exceptions non-Muslim, and its religious character was indigenous (traditional or Christian). In 1983 President Jaafar Nimeiri introduced Sharia Law and reneged on the Addis Ababa Agreement's provisions for a referendum in Abyei, dividing the south into three regions. The southern regional government was dissolved. President Nimeiry instituted a bold Islamification campaign, transforming Sudan into a Muslim Arab state. Immediately mutinies occurred throughout the south and rebel forces grew. I joined the movement's ranks in 1983-2005.

1972 Agreements Terminated (Dishonoured) by Former President Gaafar Nimeiry
In 1983 President Gaafar Nimeiry declared all Sudan an Islamic state under Shari'a law, including the non-Islamic majority southern region. The Southern Sudan Autonomous Region was abolished on the 5th

of June 1983, ending the Addis Ababa Agreement. This initiated the Second Sudanese Civil War (1983–2005).

In May 16, 1983 a number of mutinies broke out in the barracks of the Sudanese army in the southern regions, most notably in Bor. These mutineers would form the nucleus of the SPLA. By June 1983 the majority of mutineers had moved to Ethiopia, or were on their way towards Gambella. The Ethiopian government decided to support the nascent SPLA as a means of revenge for the Sudanese government support of Eritrean rebels.

The SPLA was led by Commander-in-Chief John Garang de Mabior and struggled for a united and secular Sudanese state. Garang stated that the struggle of the South Sudanese was the same as that of marginalized groups in the north, such as the Nuba and Fur peoples. Until 1985, the SPLA directed its public denouncements of the Sudanese government specifically at Nimeiri. During the years that followed, SPLA propaganda denounced the Khartoum government as a family affair that played on sectarian tensions. The SPLA denounced the introduction of sharia law in September 1983.

War in the 1980s
In the village of Bilpam, the first full-fledged SPLA battalion graduated in 1984. The name 'Bilpam' would carry a great symbolic importance for the SPLA for years to come, as the epicentre of the uprising. After Bilpam, other SPLA training camps were established at Dimma, Bonga and Panyido.

In the mid-1980s an SPLA armed struggle had blocked the development projects of the Sudanese government, such as the Jonglei Canal and the Bentiu Oil Fields.

The SPLA launched its first advance in Equatoria in 1985-1986. During this campaign, the SPLA were confronted by a number of pro-government militias. The conduct of SPLA forces was chaotic, with many atrocities against the civilian population. The SPLA drove out around 35,000 Ugandan refugees (that had settled in Equatoria since the early 1980s) back into Uganda.

The SPLA had a complicated relationship with the Anyanya II. Anyanya II forces blocked the expansion of the SPLA between 1984 and 1987, as Anyanya II attacked SPLA recruits heading towards the SPLA based in Ethiopia. Anyanya II also attacked civilians believed to be SPLA supporters. The conflict between Anyanya II and SPLA had a political dimension, as Anyanya II sought to build an independent South Sudanese state. The SPLA did however try to win over the leaders of Anyanya II to their fold. The Anyanya II commander Gordon Kong Chuol aligned with the SPLA in late 1987. Other sectors of Anyanya II would follow his example over the coming years, rendering the remainder of Anyanya II (allied with the Sudanese government) marginalized.

Another force which confronted the SPLA were the Murahaleen militias in northern Bahr el-Ghazal. Warfare between the SPLA and Muraleheen began in 1987. By 1988 the SPLA controlled most of northern Bahr el-Ghazal. Unlike the Anyanya II, however, the Murahaleen had no political ambitions.

Political Openings
The SPLA boycotted the 1986 elections. In half of the constituencies of southern Sudan elections could not be held due to the SPLA boycott. In September 1989, the RCC invited different sectors to a 'National Dialogue Conference'. The SPLA refused to attend.

On November 15th, 1988 the SPLA entered into an alliance with the DUP. The two parties had agreed on the lifting of the state of emergency and abolition of sharia law. The press release was made public through an announcement on Radio SPLA. After the DUP rejoined the government, a ceasefire with the SPLA was achieved. After the elections, negotiations between the SPLA and Sadiq al-Mahdi had started but the talks were aborted as the SPLA shot down a civilian airplane. 60 people were killed in the attack.

With the NIF coup d'état in 1989, all peace talks ended. The SPLA launched a major offensive between 1989 and the fall of the Ethiopian Derg government in 1991. They captured various towns, such as Bor, Waat, Yambio, Kaya, Kajo-Kaji, Nimule, Kapoeta, Torit, Akobo and Nasir. By the middle of 1991, the SPLA controlled most parts of southern Sudan with the exception of the major garrison towns (Juba, Yei, Malakal and Wau). Between January 21 and January 29, 1990, the SPLA shelled Juba town. SPLA forces also moved into the Nuba Mountains and the southern parts of the Blue Nile State. In comparison with its 1985-1986 offensive in Equatoria, the conduct of the SPLA was now more orderly.

1991: Setback and Split

The downfall of the Derg government in Ethiopia in May 1991 caused a major set-back. The Ethiopian government had provided the SPLA with military supplies, training facilities and safe-haven for bases during 18 years. Soon after the change of government in Ethiopia, the SPLA accompanied hundreds of thousands of refugees back into Sudan.

A split in SPLA had simmered since late 1990, as Lam Akol and Riek Machar began to question Garang's leadership. Lam Akol began secretly contacting SPLA officers to join his side, particularly amongst the Nuer people and Shilluk people. The situation deteriorated after the fall of the Derg. As the Derg regime crumbled, Lam Akol published a document titled 'Why Garang Must Go Now'. The split was made public on August 28th, 1991, in what became known as the Nasir Declaration. The dissidents called for democratization of the SPLA as well as a stop to human rights abuses. Moreover, the dissidents called for an independent South Sudan (in contrast to the SPLA line of creating a united and secular Sudan). Kong Coul joined the rebellion. The 'SPLA-Nasir' was joined by the SPLA forces in Ayod, Waat, Adok, Abwong, Ler and Akobo. A period of chaos reigned inside the SPLA, as it was not clear which units sided with Garang and which units sided with SPLA-Nasir. Garang issued a statement through the SPLA radio communications system, denouncing the coup. Nine out of eleven (excluding himself) SPLA/M PMHC members sided with Garang. The mainstream SPLA led by John Garang was based in Torit. The two SPLA factions fought each other, which included attacks on civilians in the home turf of their opponents.

Battles of 1992

As of 1992 the Sudanese government launched a major offensive against the SPLA, which was weakened by the split with SPLA-Nasir. The SPLA lost control of Torit (where they were headquartered), Bor, Yirol, Pibor, Pochalla and Kapoeta. The SPLA made two attacks on Juba in June to July 1992. The SPLA nearly captured the town. After the attacks, the Sudanese government forces committed harsh reprisals against the civilian population. Summary executions of suspected SPLA collaborators were carried out. On September 27th, 1992, the deputy commander-in-chief of the SPLA, William Nyuon, defected and took a section of fighters with him. The SPLA re-captured Bor on November 29, 1991.

Mid-1990s

During the CPA era, SPLA officers were part of a Joint Integrated Unit. As of the mid-1990s, the majority of the population of Southern Sudan lived in areas under the control of either the mainstream SPLA or SPLA-Nasir.

2005 Peace Deal

In 2004, a year before the peace deal, the Coalition to Stop Child Soldiers estimated that there were between 2,500 and 5,000 children serving in the SPLA.

Following the signing of the CPA, a transformation process of the SPLA began. This process was actively supported through funding from the United States. In 2005, John Garang restructured the top leadership of the SPLA, with a Chief of General Staff, Lt. Gen. Oyay Deng Ajak, and four Deputy Chiefs of General Staff; Maj. Gen. Salva Mathok Gengdit (Administration), Maj. Gen. Bior Ajang Aswad (Operations), Maj. Gen. James Hoth Mai (Logistics) and Maj. Gen. Obuto Mamur Mete (Political and Moral Orientation).

Everyone goes through periods of struggle in all areas of life. Obviously when life is hard and you're in a challenging season, you will struggle to get through. During the second Sudanese civil war, Comrade Soldiers and I were sent on multiple fronts where I received multiple gunshot wounds. After physical recovery from these gunshot wounds, I continued fighting for the country I loved so dearly.

Exilic Preparatory Schools
I went to Zinck/ Gambella from 1988-89, as well as Commando Training Technical Kkills for Enlisted Service Members. This linked to multiple lasers basic training and included a rigorous physical fitness program. It also built mental strength and knowledge of military history and tactics (commonly referred to as "commando training"). The Commando Training Wing (CTW) is one of two training wings in the School of Commandos of the Ethiopia Army in Ethiopia. After completing advanced training camp, recruits receive additional training specific to their career field. This type of training is known as Advanced Training (AT). It includes classroom instruction at skill-training school as well as field exercises.

Elementary Displaced School Courses
From 1993-1999, I went to Ame-Lobone-Natinga-Narus-Newland, Gambella Ethiopia, and Kakuma, Kenya preparatory schooling for continuing Educational Programs. These were a collection of fun and entertaining elementary school lessons to help me. My expert teachers guided me through a variety of essential elementary school topics,

from math to language arts and much more. Primary Source offers a rich variety of professional development programs for home-schooling educators. It includes seminars and workshops courses for more flexible learning opportunities, and free seminars that are open to the public, that added more value to my educational journey.

How did I progress in my academic journey? Below is an overview of my educational path highlighting the shifting societal attitudes over the decades; the disablers and enablers, in the hope it might inspire others to fight forward.

In 1997 we were sent to Dimma Ethiopia by the Church, and I was later ordained into the gospel ministry in 1999. Eventually God used an American (Steve Harriett) with African Christian Missions International (ACMI) to encourage and assist me to pursue further studies. This led me in 2000 to move to the refugee camp in Kakuma with my family where I received more pastoral training. After finishing college at Thika, ISOM Kenya, God led me to start a new ministry in 2004 and I joined hands with other Sudanese Church leaders to train Sudanese pastors through International School of Missions (ISOM). This is a ministry I continue to fulfil along with my shepherding responsibilities in the Anglican Church of South Sudan.

In 2004, God then rose other godly men to assist me and began my Bachelor of Arts in Bible and Theology at International Christian Ministries (ICM) Seminary in Kitale, Kenya, currently known as Africa Theological Seminary. I graduated in 2008. Beginning in 2011, I was accepted at Shepherds Theological Seminary in Cary, North Carolina, U.S.A. and graduated in 2013 with a Master of Art in Christian Ministry. So, 50 years after I was born and after nearly 27 years of hard work, my dream of achieving a doctorate has finally been fulfilled. Everything I studied in the program is directly relevant to what I do on a daily basis. I plan to put what I've learned to fine use, becoming a better college learner and applying my newfound research skills to answer the many questions I have. Again, I anticipate that the degree will expand my probabilities to consult and remain active in my profession after retirement.

My last hope is one day I would like to become a useful resource in my African continent as a professional in education. My country, the world's newest nation, has been fleeing war and many people became refugees for decades. Many generations missed educational privilege. Many people did not have educational opportunities because of the life they had to go through. I was once like these people and was not happy with my situation. Therefore, I hope to be able to help make a difference in these people's lives so that their dream may come true as any other person in the world.

In early late February 2018, at the age of 50, I completed a PhD in sociology of higher education – living proof that it's never too late to take the next step in your education! Like that of so many of our communities in our continent, my educational journey has not always been smooth or direct. It has been marked by challenges, sacrifice and detours. Looking back, I can say that it has been a journey that I will never disappoint.

Advanced degrees have provided career possibilities I would not have had otherwise, along with the community benefits that await fulfilment. Advanced education expands the way you look at and think about the world.

I join hands with a wide variety of people – many of whom are smarter than me – in order to gain self-confidence, build critical interpersonal skills and broaden my network. In the end, I achieve satisfaction from completing things that are unspecified or challenging.

Bishop Elijah Abuoi Arok, 2023

Doctor of Social and Human Studies
Atlantic International University
Honolulu, Hawaii, USA

Elijah Abuoi Arok

Master of Arts in Church Ministries
Shepherds Theological Seminary
Cary, Raleigh, North Carolina, USA

Bachelor of Arts in Bible and Theology
International Christian Ministries
Kitale, Kenya

ABSTRACT

This paper is to discuss the changing world order on global capability and the sociocultural shifts that would herald a global economy to double its amount in size by 2050. It is now estimated that population data would be stripped. India's economy rivals that of China and the US, and while Fusion power is nearing commercial availability, "Energy Islands" shall remain widespread along with Deep Ocean mining. The transformation in technology means virtual telepathy is dominating personal communications, while Biorepository and genomic information systems are transforming healthcare.

"Globalisation" is a contemporary term used in academic and non-academic contexts which describes a late twentieth and early twenty first century condition of economic, social, and political interdependence across cultures, societies, and regions, precipitated by an unprecedented expansion of capitalism on a global scale. The global rural population is expected to decrease by 0.6 billion and as a result of urbanisation. There are various pros and cons of urbanisation, which would result in: a focused population might make it, and large groups would have access to easier supply of resources with modern infrastructure for energy and water setups. Similarly, the levels of exposure to air pollution will be higher in slums or ghettos, with serious concerns for human health and wellbeing.

Keywords: Global economy Shifts; GDP; Economic growth, Materialism, Spiritual Erosion of National Pride and Identity, International Business, Economic Poverty, Superstitious beliefs, Drug/Alcohol Abuse, Single Parent Households, Religion, Education Disparity, Cultural globalisation, Obesity, Caste discrimination, Gender discrimination, Transnational Corporations, States, Global Production Networks/Health and Safety.

INTRODUCTION

A change as a result of Mass global economic shifts will be reflected by huge number of nations shifting towards economic change globally. By the year 2050, it is believed that 2.8 billion more people than the population that exists today are projected to relocate and live urban areas; this would include nearly 70% of the world's population. The various uncertainties surrounding the probability of policy options that counts in terms of political and public support, technological potential or costs should address sanitation through simulations of a various policy variants. Key environmental challenges include:

a. climate change
b. biodiversity
c. water and health
d. environment

The World's glaring domestic product (GDP) is anticipated to nearly increase fourfold over the next four decades. In the year 2050 it is expected that the OECD's share of the global economy is likely to drop from 54% in 2010 to less than 32%. Meanwhile, the share of Brazil, Russia, India, Indonesia, China and South Africa (BRIICS) as shown in Figure 1 is projected to grow to more than 40%. The US economy which has been the leading one in the world, in measures of GDP and based on the purchasing power parity exchange rates (PPPs), is being overtaken by China since 2012. Simultaneously, the GDP of India is projected to surpass that of the United States before 2040.

John Hawksworth and Danny Chan of PricewaterhouseCoopers in their report projected that the G7, which include: the US, Japan, Germany, the UK, France, Italy and Canada, plus Australia, South Korea and Spain which are now identified as having advanced economies will be replaced with the seven largest emerging market economies. They are referred to collectively as the E7 and include China, India, Brazil, Russia, Indonesia, Mexico and Turkey. Political changes are being witnessed and a warning was announced by the American President Donald Trump that the United States of America would be witness a "massive rescission ahead".

China is striving to lead the world in environmental sustainability. Back in 2009 it outpaced the United States in terms of clean energy investments and finance for the first time; its total reached $34.6 billion, almost double that of the US's $18.6 billion. While in March 2014 China led the US on a clean energy investment. For the fourth time in five years, the balance of economic power is shifting. After almost a century of dominance, the US economy has slipped down the growth rankings, and its influence over the global economy is decreasing. Economic growth in Europe is also sluggish and fragile. Yet many non-OECD countries, such as China and India,are enjoying sustained economic growth. Trade liberalisations, economic reforms, movement of capital and technology transfer are driving this growth, which is making emerging market economies increasingly important players in international finance.

In time they might well come to dominate the global economy, just as OECD countries do today. New export markets, trade relations, business models and cultural ties that better suit this redrawn economic map will no doubt emerge. The last decade shows a quadrupling of US exports to India, as well as significant growth in US investment in India. As the flow of migrants, investments and ideas from the global South increases, their influence over international politics and culture will also be transformative. However, while it is clear that global economic power is shifting, there are no guarantees that it will be a smooth transition.

In 2014, the Chinese economy overtook the United States economy to become the largest in the world, according to one measure. China now accounts for 16.5% of the global economy when measured in real purchasing-power terms, compared with 16.3% for the US. Growth in the Asia-Pacific Economic Cooperation (APEC) region has traditionally been driven by exports. However, the economies of China, Malaysia, the Philippines, Peru and Chile grew by more than 5% in 2012 despite experiencing steep declines in exports relative to their GDPs US$102 billion was spent.

AFRICA'S FIRST LIGHT RAIL SYSTEM

The first line, which opened in September 2015, connects manufacturing and industrial areas in the south with the city center's state buildings, businesses and the headquarters of the African Union. A second line connecting eastern and western districts of the city opened in November 2015. The first 32km line has 39 stations and took just three years to build, with 85% of the projects finance coming through a $475 million loan from the Export Import Bank of China. In addition to investment, the project relied heavily on engineering expertise from the China Railway Group (CREC) to construct and carry out the ongoing operation of the line. The UN has classified the project as environmentally friendly as it will have its own independent 160MW grid, powered by four gas-fueled substations. The first 32km line has 39 stations and took just three years to build, with 85% of the projects finance coming through a $475 million loan from the Export Import

Bank of China. In addition to investment, the project relied heavily on engineering expertise from the China Railway Group (CREC) to construct and carry out the ongoing operation of the line.

IMPLICATIONS

Increasing interdependence affects state power as trade growth changes the ability to disrupt or deny access. Global economic shifts have a significant influence over global politics and have impact on the other trends shaping our globalised world, such as the growth of the middle class, increasing inequality, and the role and influence of global governance and business in society. As the influence and economic activity of developing nation's increases, new markets, competitors and demands will alter patterns of trade, changing which goods are transported where. This growth in influence will also bring sweeping cultural changes to the global business and economic landscape. The shift to distributed energy generation will impact the global economy by reducing energy costs, reducing the impacts of fossil fuels, and increasing economic productivity worldwide.

SOCIAL ETHICS IN CIVILISATION

The meaning of social ethics: Social Ethics is a rule that concerned with social policies as well as with the detailed examination of the elements or structure of right and wrong in human relations. Social ethics is relevant in a society and sometimes has a life of its own. It is a distinguishing quality that appears hanging on the culture and customs applicable in areas where a community is in residence. The culture is still influenced more by the mindset of the local congregation as well and geographical conditions in which congregations live. The importance of social ethics: As we know that in every society there is certain prevailing communal moral principles. To the same extent, every individual who lives with members of the society must be willing to accept all kinds of regulations and principles governing conduct. Every action we take must be in accordance with the prevailing social order in the area. This applies globally wherever we live.

Examples of social ethics: Here are some examples of social ethics in the congregation from various regions: In Java primarily Central Java, people must bow when walking in front of others, especially older ones. Social principles governing conduct is valid for the purpose as a symbol of treating an individual in a dignified manner. When walking into someone's home, people have knock on the door and wait for permission to enter. The aim is to respect the one's space and the existence of the host. When emitting wind, it should be noisily from the stomach through the mouth while eating. This is an example of social ethics as opposed to Indonesian customs.

In Korea wilayah if any friends or close relatives who invited you to eat together then belch, this is a form of formal public acknowledgement of allegiance, but in regions like Europe when people do a belch in the time or after a meal is considered very ill-mannered. The justification for an action is that it can hinder with mood because it put an end to the noise that can bring a sense of disgust. Distinctly different from the first example of social ethics is in Java. People who are get advice from parents should lower their face.

But in Europe, when there are people who express feelings look at each other's face, as a form of attention, to signal the communications that are underway. So, God created people in his own image and in the image of God he created them, male and female. To be created as a human is therefore to be inherently social, yet Adam and Eve sinned, against divine law and succeeding generations have been sinning ever since.

This transgression introduces strife into the social sphere. As God compensates for the faults and restores this world, there is need for good judgment plus an understanding of the ethics that go into living life as social creatures by nature.

A set of moral principles, especially ones affirming a specified group, field, or form of conduct within a society, determine what is deemed right and just and noble. The Bible has much to say concerning social ethics, in its call to justice and righteousness in the Old Testament and in Christ's ethical teaching in the New Testament, the Scripture teaches how those created in God's image are to live together in this world. In a clear manner, The Scripture views social ethics as crucial to the picture it portrays of what human life is meant to be (Amos 5:24; Gen. 18:19; 1 Sam. 15:22–23). The Lord's yearn for righteousness to be practiced by the world, and by his own people. This reflects his own character: "I am the Lord who practices steadfast love, justice/ righteousness in the earth. For in these things, I delight" (Jer. 9:24). God is passionate for equity and harmony among people. Jesus' words in the Great Commandment bring a fitting New Testament summary, as he instructs his people to love God and to love others, declaring that such vertical and horizontal love sums up the entire Old Testament ethic (Matt. 22:37–40; Lev. 19:18; Deut. 6:5; Rom. 13:8–10). Social ethics is factual in another respect, because it is portrayed in the Scripture as that which pushes God's people to obey the law by genuinely considering the need of others to be just as important as their own need (Lev. 19:18; Matt. 19:19; 22:39; Rom. 13:9; Gal. 5:14; James 2:8). Indeed, Christians are called to put the welfare of others ahead of their own needs as the Bible stated (Rom. 12:10).

When we consider Issues of Global Social Ethics, taking into consideration the ethical dimension of corporate life in this sinful world, primarily corporate life as the redeemed people of God, we will turn to consider a handful of pressing issues concerning social ethics. In what follows we will consider tribalism, hunger, slavery, human trafficking, and occultism. In considering each of these we are asking what the Bible has to say about such pressing global concerns.

What can we learn from Scripture? Tribalism continues to be a serious problem across communities. Tribalism is a social, immoral act considered to be a transgression against divine law that has to do with the exaltation of one ethnic society above others. It involves a strong in-community loyalty and ethnic connection that manifests itself not only in separation of one's own ethnic society from the rest but also in unfair elevation of individuals in an in-community. Tribalism in its current form is not just about tribal group strictly speaking but can be detected in communities across nations. While the scripture affirms ultimately rejoices in racial dissimilarity (Rev. 5:9–10; 7:9–10), it also shows equality of all societies regardless of ethnicity (Eph. 2:14–18). In Jesus, there is only one community, one nation, one "tribe": "There is neither Jew nor Greek, there is neither slave nor free, there is no male and female, for all people are one in Christ Jesus. And if we are Christ's, then we are Abraham's offspring, heirs according to promise" (Gal. 3:28–29). The scripture teaches that Christ has torn down the wall of disunity and has brought Jew and Gentile into one body (Eph. 2:14; 3:6). Scripture teaches us that a close similarity in Christ supersedes all other similarities. Moreover, all people are created in the image of God (Gen. 1:26–27; 9:6). As we acquire knowledge to resist the elevation of ourselves or our ethnicity, which our nature of sin advocates, we can joyfully exult in the wonder of being included in one community as the Christian Bible encourages, known as the "body" of Christ (Eph. 4:3–7).

Disunity in the world is a problem and is growing at high alarming rates every day. Today, around the globe, communities are suffering from an insufficient amount of the healthiest things to eat. Across the world four elements are agreed upon as the main causes of global strife. These elements are namely: inadequate economic systems; 1) hunger 2) poverty; 3) interpersonal and inter-ethnic conflict; 4) past existing hunger, which is to increase in extent, as a structural flaw.

One element for this desire for food is that it often links up to other ethical issues, such as poverty, political dishonesty, hurtful economic systems, and global conflict. The problem of global suffering therefore, generated by sins such as exploitation, indifference, and greed. While secular social theory can comment to an extent, only the biblical world view can get to the root cause of much of the situation around global issues where lack of food is a problem.

Another factor as to why it is well founded to consider global hunger an ethical problem for debate or discussion is found in the Bible. The Bible explains that there is an ethical loyalty on the part of God's people who have plenty food to share with persons who are in need (Lev. 19:18; 25:35; Deut. 15:7–8; 26:12–13; Prov. 19:17). Christ went as far as to explain that when believers provide food and drink to people who need help, they are giving food and drink to Christ himself (Matt. 25:31–46). On one hand, we must recall that the greatest need of every person is to be forgiven and made an heir of eternal life through Christ Jesus. This is "of first of great significance" (1 Cor. 15:3).

Thus, worry and safekeeping for the poor and the hungry is not to alter but rather to complement the teaching of the Scripture. Yet we must also remember that to teach the bible without "linking" it with works of love is to render such a scriptural proclamation hollow and harmful to the name of Christ (Titus 2:7–8; compare 1 John 3:17–18). In all of this we are heartened by the Bible's teachings that God draws near to those who are suffering in hunger and identifies with them in their affliction (Ps. 9:12; 82:3–4; 140:12; Isa. 57:15).

Slavery and human trafficking: Slavery and human trafficking are complementary. Trafficking is perhaps the superlative, vast form of slavery around the global today. Anytime a person is held captive by another against the captive's will, this is slavery.

Trafficking includes the buying and selling of the enslaved. Whereas slavery is supposed to have ended over a period of one hundred year ago, today there are close 30 million slaves worldwide (More than twice the number of slaves transported during the entire trans-Atlantic slave trade). This figure includes forms such as chattel slavery in southern Sudan and Mauritania, child "Carpet slaves" in India, shackled laborers in Pakistan, cane cutters in the Dominican Republic, and those (especially girls) who are trafficked as sex slaves all around the world. The Scripture addresses the social justice issues which occur globally, nationally, regionally, locally, and within groups. These issues are a result of unequal wealth and resource distribution, unfair treatment of individuals with differing traits (race, culture, sexual orientation, religion, etc), and laws that support segregation. All humans are created in God's image and therefore have intrinsic value. God not only created all people in his image, but he also delights in all people (Gen. 1:26–31; John 3:16; 1 Tim. 2:1–4). Universal human immoral acts considered to be a transgression against divine law does not mean that God is unable able to delight in his fine creation, however profoundly spoiled through human transgression it may be. Again, God instructs his people to love others and especially those in need (Matt. 7:12; Luke 10:25–37; Rom. 13:8–10). Also, God hates slavery and human trafficking: "Whoever steals a man and sells him, and anyone found in possession of him, shall be put to death" (Ex. 21:16). The New Testament lists slave traders among "the ungodly and sinners" and puts them in the same category as practitioners of murder and other grievous sins (1 Tim. 1:8–10). The biblical doctrine of salvation customarily portrays us as slaves who have been freed from the most serious, slavery of all—slavery to sin and death (Rom. 6:15–23; Gal. 4:3, 8; Titus 3:3–7; 2 Pet. 2:19). Therefore, anyone experienced God's gift of salvation and freedom must accept that enslaving another human being goes against the will of God. Christians should therefore pray for and advocate on behalf of those caught up in slavery and human trafficking (Prov. 31:8–9; James 2:14–17; 5:16).

WILL OF GOD

One theme that all parts of Bible take up in one way or another is the will of God. God's will is as vast as his entire plan for creation, and from the standpoint of objective content, it seems to be settled and unchanging. Old and New Testament writers can thus refer to God's will as if its existence is accepted by all. Though it may seem to have the character of a broad blueprint, in practical applications it is expressed in specific terms. God's will can also be viewed from an active side as His conscious "deciding, " "willing, " and "choosing" to do something.

The Old Testament: The affirmation from the Old Testament that there exists with the God of Israel a will that is resolute and bears on his actions and the life of his people is made clear in all parts of the Old Testament. The impression created is that he has worked and continues to interact with his creation according to a design. Psalm 135:6 announces that "the Lord does whatever pleases him." His will is also the pattern to be followed in life by his people.

The will of God is not simply a passive plan, it is the blueprint for His creation. Rather, very often the Old Testament describes God as accomplishing His will. In this we glimpse the sovereign control He exerts over nations and individuals as well as the imperturbable certainty that characterizes His will. Broadly speaking, "Our God is in heaven; he does whatever pleases him" (Psalm 115:3 ; 135:6). Specifically, God's will applies to nations (Isa 48:14) as well as to decisions made about individuals (1 Sam 2:25). What God has planned, will come to pass. Suitably, the development of understanding the will of God in the Old Testament reveals that God in one sense may be seen as the initiator in the execution of His will and that this may involve the events that make up human history. Human history is never regarded as beyond His control. This includes not only the sweeping developments that affect whole nations, but also the specific events that touch individual lives. For this reason, the people are to align their lives with and do the will of God. Psalm 40:8 becomes a programmatic statement in this respect: "I desire to do your will, O my God; your law is within my heart." In this text the psalmist brings together two essential elements in describing the ideal life of obedience to God. God requires certain patterns of behavior in response to His covenant. The law is the articulation of the ethical requirements of God's will. This pattern is also taken up in the "new covenant" passage of Jeremiah 31:31-34: doing God's law (will) is the essence of the appropriate life of response to God's covenant. For God's will to be done, it had first to be known and understood by his people: "Teach me to do your will, for you are my God" (Psalm 143:10). Through Moses, the judges, and the prophets, God made his will known and led the people in applying it in everyday situations. In one case, the application of God's will to a specific situation meant putting away foreign wives(Ez.10:11). When people act, it is to be done in awareness that God's will is to be the guide and that it cannot be thwarted (Job 42:2). Thus before taking action, David said to the people, "If it seems good to you, and if it is the will of the Lord our God, let us " (1 Chron 13:2).The concept of God's will is developed specifically along theological lines, in reference to salvation, in the servant passages in Isaiah. God selected Cyrus to carry out his purpose, which would allow the city of Jerusalem and the temple to be rebuilt (44:28). Here God's will is executed in a historical event; moreover, that act is stereological for through it God's people experience salvation. The song of the Suffering Servant reveals that "it was the Lord's will to crush him" (53:10). This expression of the will of God, His resolute plan, however, takes its meaning from 42:1-9 and 49:1-7, which makes it clear that God's purpose is the deliverance of Israel and the Gentile nations, and that somehow the suffering of the Servant plays a role within this plan. Again, historical events are seen to have significance as they develop out of the determined will of God. Finally, the executions of God's salvation, the "mission" of the redemption of Israel and the nations, is linked to the proclamation of God's efficacious words: "so is my word that goes out from my mouth."

    The will of God as a superstructure for God's intervention in the affairs of humankind and for all of life was a belief that shaped much of the early church's outlook on theology and life. In addition to the influence of the Old Testament, Jesus' own life, ministry, and teaching undoubtedly provided a formative influence.

Jesus' life and teaching, as recorded in the Gospels, bear witness to the importance of the concept of the will of God and is important in understanding his place and that of his followers in redemptive history. Jesus modeled for his disciples a life lived in perfect conformity with God's will and demonstrated that this life did not always take the easy course. The poignant Gethsemane scene, recorded by Matthew, Mark, and Luke (with slight variations), depicts this most clearly. As Jesus prayed to the Father, he acknowledged both the strength of his own will and his commitment to God's: "My Father, if it is possible, may this cup be taken from me. Yet not as I will, but as you will My Father, if it is not possible for this cup to be taken away unless I drink it, may your will be done" (Matthew 26:39 Matthew 26:42 ; cf. Mark 14:36 ; Luke 22:42). Both Jesus and the Gospel writers knew that God's will concerning the Messiah's death was specific. But John especially characterizes the whole of Jesus' ministry in terms of conformity with the will of God. At one point Jesus said to his disciples, "My food is to do the will of him who sent me" (John 4:34). His ministry is described as the outworking of God's will: "I can do nothing on my own. As I hear, I judge; and my judgment is just, because I seek to do not my own will but the will of him who sent me" (5:30 ; 6:38-40).

If Jesus was to do God's will, so were his disciples. The prayer that Jesus taught them made God's will a central concern in the life of discipleship. They were to petition God that his kingdom might come and his will be done on earth as it is in heaven (Matt 6:10). The coming of the kingdom, God's power in Christ and then, through the Holy Spirit, in his church, would mean the manifestation of God's will on the earthly plane. The implication contained in the petition extends to the conduct of the disciples, as the Sermon on the Mount's context reveals. Thus, the message of the kingdom of God and the concept of God's will are joined together. In fact, kinship with Jesus is demonstrated not by correct doctrine but by doing God's will (Matt 12:50 ; Mark 3:35). Equally, membership in God's kingdom is demonstrated not by good intentions but by the actual execution of God's will (Matt 7:21 ; 21:31 ; Luke 12:47). Obedience to the will of God challenges and supersedes legalistic obedience to religious rules, which through concretisation have become meaningless and even hinder the pursuit of knowledge of God (John 9:31). Ultimately, the readiness of an individual to acknowledge and then do God's will determines whether that person will be able to apprehend the truth of Jesus (John 7:17).

In the thought of the early church, as represented by Paul and other New Testament writers, Is that the will of God continues to have a prominent place.

God's Will and the Direction of Life: At its most basic level, belief in an all-encompassing will of God means the belief that things are moving in a direction such as Romans 1:9-10 ("I remember you in my prayers at all times; and I pray now at last by God's will the way may be opened for me to come to you"), Romans 15:32 ("so that by God's will I may come to you"), and jas 4:15 ("Instead, you ought to say, If it is the Lord's will, we will live and do this or that'"). The early Christians held that God's will might supervene in the lives of his people and bring a change to human plans, for God's will cannot be resisted (Rom 9:19). Consequently, the Christian's aim is to live according to the perfect will of God and to pray according to it (1 John 5:14). In many cases this may exceed the ability of the believer, but the Holy Spirit is capable, who "intercedes for the saints in accordance with God's will" (Rom 8:27).

God's Will and the Plan of Salvation: Receiving special emphasis is the place of the plan of salvation within God's will. The adoption as children (Eph 1:5) and inheritance of the blessings of redemption (v. 11) are according to God's counsel and will. The basis of salvation, the crucifixion of God's son Jesus, is explicitly described as the outworking of God's will (Acts 2:23 ; 4:28 ; Gal 1:4). In this way, Jesus' death becomes integral to God's plan, rather than being an unforeseen event to be viewed whatever way possible. Furthermore, the redemptive will of God, which began long ago in the promises to Abraham, has proceeded without change through each stage of the plan (Heb 6:17). Like Abraham, others played significant roles in the outworking of God's will to save (Acts 13:36); at each point God's will was determinative and could not be circumvented (Luke 7:30). Paul viewed his own call to apostleship, which was to bring salvation to the Gentiles (Titus 1:1), in precisely these terms. Nearly all his letters emphasize that it was God's will that established him in his ministry (1 Cor 1:1 ; 2 Cor 1:1 ; 1Col 1:1 ; 2 Tim 1:1 ; cf. Gal 1:1 ; 1 Tim 1:1 ; Titus 1:1).Does the New Testament teach that it is God's will that all be saved, and therefore none will be lost? Two passages relate God's will to the expansiveness of the salvation plan. 1Timothy 2:3-4 states, "God our Savior wills all men to be saved and to come to a knowledge of the truth." 2 Peter 3:9 expresses a similar sentiment: "The Lord does not will anyone to perish but that everyone might come to repentance." It should be emphasized that neither text says that all will be saved regardless of their disposition toward the gospel. In the first text, "to come to a knowledge of the truth" is a rule expressed in symbols that means to make a rational decision about the gospel, that is, to respond to the gospel message. The second text similarly relates God's will to save the all-inclusive "anyone" to the volitional element involved in repentance. Consequently, while these texts tell us that God's will to save extends to all people, and that he desires to save rather than to condemn, they do not remove the necessary element of the faith-response to the gospel.

The Christian Life as a Continuous Response to God's Will: God's will applies to every part of the church's and believer's lives. The strong link of the term with God's will makes it almost certain that in such cases (Rom 2:18 ; James 4:15) it stands as an abbreviation for God's will. Christian living and "doing the will of God" are one and the same and are not to be separated. In general terms, the summary of faithful Christian living, given by the writer of Hebrews, is "Doing the will of God": "For you need endurance, so that when you have done the will of God, you may receive what was promised" (10:36). John describes the life of faithfulness, which demonstrates true Christianity, similarly, as doing the will of God (1 John 2:17). Viewed more specifically, for the slave, being a Christian within the social institution of slavery called for obedience to the master as this was doing the will of God from the heart (Eph 6:6). Suffering as Christians is an aspect of Christian existence that corresponds to God's will (1 Peter 4:19).Other specific applications of God's will reveal clearly how it is relevant to all areas of human life. First Thessalonians 4:3 states that God's will is "our sanctification, " which Paul then goes on to apply in the specific principle "abstain from fornication." Later in the same letter the will of God is said to be thankfulness in all situations (5:18). It is God's will that a Christian's conduct remove any cause for slander by unbelievers (1 Peter 2:15). Doing good deeds and sharing what we have with one another are "acceptable to God, " that is, accords with his will (Heb 13:15-16). Finally, the will of God, which Paul desires his people to know and do according to the Romans 12:2, is spelled out specifically in terms of mutual service among Christians in the passage that follows. In no case do the specifics or even any combination of them exhaust or fully describe the will of God. They merely show the directions its practical application will take. The will of God must be done by Christians if they are genuine Christians, but for this to occur two things are required. First, it must be taught and understood. Paul, for one, was chosen by God to know God's will (Acts 22:14). He also endeavored to make all of God's will (counsel) known, in the form of both theology and Christian ethics (Acts 20:27). His prayer for believers was that they "be filled with a knowledge of God's will" (Col 1:9 ; 4:12). And he admonished foolish believers for trying to gain an understanding of God's will (Eph 5:17).

Second, God must equip the believer to be able to execute the divine will in appropriate behavior. Human inability continues to coexist alongside divine sovereignty. This means that God must give the enlightenment necessary for the believer to perceive what the will of God is(Col 1:9). "Now may the God of peace, who brought back from the dead our Lord Jesus make you complete in everything good so that you may do his will, working among us that which is pleasing in his sight" (Heb 13:20-21 ;).

The Will of God and Guidance: Within the church today there are various views about how specifically God's will may be known and followed in matters of life's decisions. In the Old Testament God provided tools for discerning his direction in various situations. At times he "Spoke," whether in dreams, through the burning bush, or in the "still small voice" that came to Elijah. In the New Testament similar events of guidance are recorded. It becomes clear that the church and individual believers are to seek to know God's will and base their actions on it. While a general pattern emerges that tells us that God is in control of his church, the whole world and is interested in each aspect of his children's lives, we are not told specifically whether God will give us a "yes" or "no" to each question we might ask. Much of the biblical teaching about His will pertains to behavior and his plan of salvation. Regarding the first, "seeking" his will means (1) learning what God's Word says about aspects of our response to him and, (2) in concert with the church, determining how that teaching is to be applied in new historical and cultural contexts.

SINGLE PARENTS FOR ECONOMIC INEQUALITY

A single parent refers to a parent who has one or more than one child and is not living with the children's other parent. As Timothy Noah wrote in Slate years ago, the biggest changes in the American family structure took place in the '70s and '80s. They help explain why, for example, the ratio between the 90th percentile of earners and 10th percentile is higher than it was 30 years ago. The shift away from two-parent households doesn't really factor into the concentration of wealth among the 1 percent. And the rise of the 1 percent, and the 0.1 percent for that matter, is the real story when it comes to how income inequality is evolving today. In this current economy, the people of God must remember that if you honor God through your wealth, he will direct your path.

"Trust in the Lord with all your heart. Lean not on your own understanding, acknowledge him, and he will direct your path." Proverbs 3:5-6 (NIV) Learn something every day. If you only lean on your own knowledge in your life, you will not be able to grow. You must grow yourself in order to grow other people.

"Behold, I am doing something new! It's already happening; don't you recognize it? I will clear a way in the desert. I will make rivers on dry land." Isaiah 43:19 (GOD'S WORD® Translation) Sometimes your life will need to adapt as a situation pulls you in a different direction. You might need to reinvent your life, and you should not be afraid. God's always got your back.

"Do not be anxious about anything, but in everything, by prayer and petition, with thanksgiving, present your requests to God." Philippians 4:6 (NIV) One of the most important things you can do for your life is to pray every day.

"Faith without work is dead." James 2:26 (KJV) You can't just pray for success. Develop a plan and Work to carry out your plan. If you can do something about your situation, then do it. Stop making excuses, stop procrastinating, and do it! "Have I not commanded you? Be strong and courageous and do not be terrified; do not be discouraged, for the LORD your God will be with you wherever you go." Joshua 1:9. "As I think in my heart, so am I." Proverbs 23:7. "God has not given me a spirit of fear, but of power, love and sound mind."

Try hard not to be reactionary with situations, vendors or employees. Use factual information and up to date financial advice to make sound life decisions. "These things won't happen right away. Slowly, steadily, surely, the time approaches when the vision will be fulfilled. If it seems slow, do not discourage, for these things will surely come to pass. They will not be overdue a single day." Habakkuk 2:3 You need to understand that God's time is not the same as your time.

"Happy is the man who finds wisdom, and the man who gains understanding;" Proverbs 3:13. You need to be a lifelong learner in order to be successful in life. You should constantly seek to improve yourself and increase your knowledge about the situation of current activities. "I have told you these things, so that in me you may have peace. In this world you will have trouble"

It came to me while I was watching world news and I believe I was only watching the news to order to see it. Remember, whether you are religious or not you can always pray about your situation. Special Shout out to Joyce Meyer Ministries for her book The Secret Power of Speaking God's Word which gives guidance for biblical wisdom. "Single mom, may the God of hope fill you with all joy and peace in believing, so that by the power of the Holy Spirit you may abound in hope." (Romans 15:13).

May God, the source of hope, fill you with all joy and peace by means of your faith in Him, so that your hope will continue to grow by the power of the Holy Spirit (Psalm 33:22). If life feels hopeless right now, I want you to know you are not without hope because you are not alone. Jesus is with you. He loves you. He hears every prayer and sees every tear. The LORD's unfailing love and mercy continues, fresh as the morning, as sure as the sunrise. The LORD is all you have, and so in Him you put your hope. Biblical mandates have been engaging people with the life-changing message of God's Word so that hopeless single parents can stay in touch with how God is changing lives.

PREVENTING ALCOHOL AND SUBSTANCE ABUSE WITH GOD'S WORD

Drug addiction stalks the lives of million people and enslaves their victims with terrible consequences. Willful, repeated sinful behavior can cement fundamentally flawed logic and what The Scripture calls a hardening of ourhearts or being given over to "a depraved mind" (Romans 1:28). It's not that God wouldn't take us back. The Bible explicitly instructs us to refrain from getting high. Scripture specifically instructs us to avoid risking our lives. The apostle Paul writes, "Do not get drunk on wine, which leads to debauchery. Instead, be filled with the Spirit" (Ephesians 5:18). The reason Paul gives for this instruction is that consuming alcohol leads to indulging in passions without restraint, a.k.a. debauchery. He contrasts drunkenness with being filled with the Holy Spirit of God. The principle behind the passage is simply this: Stay away from stuff that will confuse your thoughts, weaken your inhibitions and make you more vulnerable to sin.

Can we think of a drug that doesn't do all those things? Whether depressant or stimulant, psychedelic or dissociative, legal or illegal, substances that mess with your mind get a poor rap in God's book: "In the end it bites like a snake and poisons like a viper. Your eyes will see strange sights and your mind imagines confusing things" (Proverbs 23:32-33). God wants our thoughts and life under His control. Did you know that God cares what we think about? In fact, Paul goes so far as to describe a war waged all over the world, fought in part for your mind: For though we live in the world, we do not wage war as the world does. The weapons we fight with are not the weapons of the world. On the contrary, they have divine power to demolish strongholds. We demolish arguments and every pretension that sets itself up against the knowledge of God, and we take captive every thought to make it obedient to Christ (2 Corinthians 10:3-5). The way we think is central to the way we live. How we think about drugs and how drugs make us think is both crucial. A drug-dazed mind can keep us from properly seeing what's right and what's wrong in many situations. The virtue in the ethics of self-control are critical for a disciple of Jesus Christ. Self-control is one of the primary virtues of the Christian life.

A WORLD OF RAPID CHANGE

In his 2004 bestseller Margin, physician and futurist Richard Swenson explains that change picked up momentum in the early part of the 20th century and the world has been rapidly accelerating ever since. The reason, he states, is that "the mathematics are different. Many of the linear lines that in the Past that described our lives well, have now disappeared continuing change exponentially. Twenty-four hours. Week after week, everything seems about the same. Meanwhile, largely unnoticed by us, history has shifted to fast forward. If linear best describes our personal lives, exponential now best describes most of historical change" (p. 40). This period of accelerating change we're now experiencing has put a strain on individuals and entire societies. In 1970, futurist Alvin Toffler described the effects of "too much change in too short a period of time" in his contemporary classic Future Shock. He predicted that people exposed to these rapid changes of modern life would suffer from "shattering stress and disorientation." They would be, in his words, "future-shocked." He predicted that people exposed to these rapid changes of modern life would suffer from "shattering stress and disorientation." They would be, in his words, "future-shocked."However according to Kurzweil, since the beginning of evolution, more complex life forms have been evolving exponentially faster, with shorter and shorter intervals between the emergence of radically new life forms, such as human beings, who have the capacity to engineer. The fear of rapid change is big today," observes Gabe Ignatow, Ph.D., a sociologist at the University of North Texas. "Many people see the changes going on in the world around us and are worried and anxious. If they also have changes going on in their personal lives maybe they lost their job or had to find a new place to live because their home was foreclosed it can all be overwhelming." What has caused our world to change so rapidly in recent years? "Ultimately, it's due to technological advances," replies Ignatow. Case in point: With the advent of the printing press in the 15th century, there was certainly a paradigm shift (a change from one way of thinking to another), but it took a century for that shift to occur.

VIOLENCE IN SCHOOLS

"Indicators of School Crime and Safety," a 2006 study by the U.S. Department of Education and United States Department of Justice revealed that public schools experiencing violent incidents increased from 71 to 81 percent over a five-year period (1999-2004).

School violence is a multi-faceted problem, making it difficult for researchers to pinpoint its causes. Many people involved in school violence suffer from mental anguish and emotional disorders after going through something traumatic. School violence has negative effects and can cause physical, mental, and emotional harm. Departments of Education and Justice, monitors school-associated violent deaths at the national level. Information is collected from media databases, police, and school officials. A case is defined as a fatal injury (e.g., homicide or suicide) that occurs (1) on school property; (2) on the way to/from school; or (3) during or on the way to/from a school sponsored event. Only violent deaths associated with U.S. elementary and secondary schools, public and private, are included. Data obtained from this study plays an important role in monitoring and assessing national trends in school-associated violent deaths and help to inform efforts to prevent fatal school violence. The Centre for Disease Control and Prevention (CDC), the U.S. Department of Education, and the U.S. Department of Justice gather and analyze data from a variety of sources to gain a more complete understanding of school violence. According to CDC's Youth Risk Behavior Survey (YRBS), nearly 8% of students had been in a physical fight on school property one or more times during the 12 months before the survey. Nationwide, about 6% of students had not gone to school at least 1 day during the 30 days before the survey because they felt they would be unsafe at school or on their way to or from school. The same study reports that the percentage of students who reported gang presence at school increased from 21 percent in 2003 to 24 percent in 2005.

MATERIALISM

Materialism is defined as "the preoccupation with material things rather than intellectual or spiritual things." If a Christian is preoccupied with material things, it is wrong. That is not to say we cannot have material things, but the obsession with acquiring and caring for "stuff" is a dangerous thing for the Christian, for two reasons.

Primarily, any preoccupation, or fascination with anything other than God is wicked, immoral and is displeasing to God. We are to "love the Lord, your God, with all your heart, and with all your soul, and with all your might" (Deuteronomy 6:5), which is, according to Jesus, the first and greatest commandment (Matthew 22:37-38). Therefore, God is the only thing we can (and should) occupy ourselves with habitually. He alone is worthy of our complete attention, love and service. To offer these things to anything, or anyone, else is idolatry. Secondly, when we perturb ourselves with the material world, we are easily drawn in by the "deceitfulness of wealth" (Mark 4:19), thinking that we will be happy or fulfilled or content if only we had more of whatever it is we are chasing. This is a lie from the father of lies, Satan. He wants us to be chasing after something he knows will never satisfy us so we will be kept from pursuing that which is the only thing that can satisfy—God Himself. Luke 16:13 tells us we "cannot serve both God and money."

We must seek to be content with what we have, and materialism is the exact opposite of that contentment. It causes us to strive for more and more and more, all the while telling us that this will be the answer to all our needs and dreams. The Bible tells us that a person's "life is not in the abundance of the things which he possesses" (Luke 12:15) and that we are to "seek first the kingdom of God and His righteousness" (Matthew 6:33). If materialism was ever to satisfy anyone, it would have been Solomon, richest king the world has ever known.

OBESITY

Obesity is a condition where a person has accumulated so much body fat that it might have a negative effect on their health. These days' people eat much more food than previous generations. This used to be the case just in developed nations; however, the trend has spread worldwide. In the USA, the consumption of calories increased from 1,542 per day for women in 1971 to 1,877 per day in 2004 and the figures for men were 2,450 in 1971 and 2,618 in 2004. Most people would expect this increase in calories to consist of fat - not so! Most of the increased food consumption has consisted of sugars. Increased consumption of sweetened drinks have contributed significantly to the raised carbohydrate intake of most young American adults over the last three decades. The consumption of fast foods has tripled over the same period. "How should a Christian view weight loss? What does the Bible say about obesity? While nothing in the Bible specifically addresses obesity and weight loss, there is much in God's Word about the importance of our health and of taking care of our bodies. God warns us against gluttony. In the Old Testament God gave specific instructions about what His people, the Israelites, were to eat (Deuteronomy 14:1–21). Most of these commands were designed to keep the Israelites from eating harmful foods that would negatively impact their health. Some of the commands were also given so God's people wouldn't imitate the habits of the idolatrous people around them. Gluttony, which is overeating or drinking to excess, is condemned in the Bible (Proverbs 23:20–21). Gluttony can lead to health risks and become a drain on one's finances. Plus, the love of food and drink can all too easily become an idol in our lives. Anything that takes the place of God or becomes our number-one focus is, by definition, an idol and thus a sin against God (Exodus 20:3–6). Proverbs 23:2 exhorts us to "put a knife to your throat if you are given to gluttony"; in other words, we are admonished to restrain our appetites. In the New Testament, Paul tells followers of Jesus Christ that their bodies are temples of the Holy Spirit (1 Corinthians 6:19–20). That being the case, we should take care of our bodies and keep them as healthy as possible. Knowing that being obesity can lead to multiple health problems, including back and knee pain and cardio-vascular complications, we should make wise choices regarding food, drink, and exercise. We should be careful not to imply that being overweight is synonymous with gluttony. That would be an over-simplification. There are indeed, medical conditions and medicines that lead to weight gain and situations that prevent proper exercise. Such circumstances require a much greater effort than the average person expends to keep one's weight under control.

If there are no extenuating circumstances, then being overweight is usually an outward sign of a life out of balance. Anxiety and depression are a couple of the most common reasons to eat out of balance. "Anxious eating" is much more common than most people realize. Of course, the Bible has plenty to say about how to deal with anxiety and depression. God repeatedly tells His children not to fear and to cast their cares upon Him (1 Peter 5:7).

Jesus taught us to seek a balance between the physical and the spiritual: "Man shall not live on bread alone, but on every word that comes from the mouth of God" (Matthew 4:4). Striving for balance in our eating habits—and balancing our physical needs with our spiritual necessities—requires wisdom. Weight loss requires more than simply desiring to lose weight. It's possible to desire something and never attain it. In the Christian life, we must make decisions that "take off the old self" and "put on the new self" (Ephesians 4:22–24). Similarly, to attain a balance in our diet, we must put aside old habits and develop new ones. Also, the Christian life teaches us that success is easier when we are sharing the journey with others. In the same way, weight loss is best accomplished with others who can provide some degree of accountability. While obesity and weight loss are valid concerns, we must be careful not to become obsessed with body image. Again, when something besides God becomes the major focus of life, it is sin.

EDUCATIONAL DISPARITY

Psychological science offers an understanding of educational disparities and strategies to address them. The organisation of schools and how students are engaged in their learning is of critical importance for the educational achievement of students across racial groups. Educational inequality is the unequal distribution of academic resources, including but not limited to; school funding, qualified and experienced teachers, books, and technologies to socially excluded communities. The Old Testament record indicates repeatedly that the success of the Hebrew community and the continuity of its culture were conditioned by the knowledge of and obedience to God's revealed law (Joshua 1:6-8).

Thus, to ensure their prosperity, growth, and longevity the people of Yahweh, Israel's mandate was one of education, diligently teaching their children to love God and to know and obey His statues and ordinances (Deut 6:1-9). Likewise, the New Testament record links the success of the church of Jesus Christ, as a worshiping community of "salt and light" reaching out to a dark world, to the teaching of sound doctrine (John 13:34-35 ; Eph 4:14 ; 1 Tim 1:10 ; Titus 2:1). Education in the Ancient near East: Since education is basic to the existence of any community or society it is only natural that certain foundational principles of education are vital properties among diverse people groups. The case is no different when we study the educational practices of the Israelites within the context of education in world of the ancient Near East.

Education in the ancient world was rooted in religious tradition and theological ideals. The goal of education was the transmission of that religious tradition, along with community mores and values, and vocational and technical skills. The by-product of this kind of education was a model citizen, loyal to family, gods, and king, upright in character, and productive in community life. More than liberally educated "free-thinkers," the important outcome of the educational system for the early communities was utilitarian, equipping people to be functional members of family and society. For the most part the teaching method was based upon rote learning. This memorisation of the curricular materials was accomplished by both oral and written recitation. Disciplined learning characterized educational instruction, with lessons taught at fixed times during the day and often for a set number of days in a month.

In addition to being teachers and drill masters, parents (in the home) and tutors (in the formal schools) also functioned as mentors and role-models, teaching by example and lifestyle. The primary agency of education in both ancient Egypt and Mesopotamia was the home, parents and elders of an extended family were responsible for the education of children. First, the emphasis upon individual personality in Hebrew faith meant that education must respect the individual and seek to develop the whole person. Second, the emphasis on the fatherhood of God in Israelite religion brought a sense of intimacy to the Creator-creature relationship and a sense of purpose and urgency to human history.

Thus, Hebrew education stressed the importance of recognizing and remembering acts and events of divine providence in history. Third, the idea of personal freedom in Hebrew religion gave men and women dignity as free moral agents in creation; likewise Hebrew education stressed the responsibility individuals have toward God and others, accountability of human behavior, and the need for disciplined training in making "right" choices. Fourth, the notion of the Israelites as a divinely chosen people encouraged fierce nationalistic overtones in Hebrew religion and education; religiously the Israelites were obligated to the demands of God's holiness in order to remain His special possession, while educationally they were obligated to instruct all nations in divine holiness and redemption as Yahweh's instrument of light to the nations. Fifth, the doctrine of human sin and sinfulness stamps both Hebrew religion and education; this introduced the concept of mediation in Israelite religion.

Education in Old Testament Times: Hebrew education was both objective (external and content oriented) and subjective (internal and personally oriented), cognitive (emphasis on the intellect) and affective (emphasis on the will and emotions), and both active (investigative and participatory) and passive (rote and reflective). Specifically, the teaching-learning process involved disciplined repetition in observation, experiential learning (doing), listening, reciting, and imitating. On occasion special guidance (directed study) as well as correction and warning were a part of the educational experience. Finally, critical thinking skills were an important educational outcome because learning had application to daily living.

Purpose: The purpose of Old Testament education is encapsulated within the revelation given to Abraham concerning the destruction of Sodom and Gomorrah. Here God bids Abraham to direct his children in "the way of the Lord."

This divine directive embodies the very essence of Hebrew education in the Old Testament, affirming the primacy of parental instruction. In addition, the verse identifies the desired goal or outcome of education: a lifestyle of doing justice and righteousness.

There was also benefit attached to this "behavior modification in Yahweh moral values" in the form of the possession of the land of promise for the Israelites who followed through on the charge to educate their children in the way of the Lord. Genesis 18:19 cryptically describes the content of Hebrew education as "the way of the Lord." What is meant by this phrase and how does it relate to the religious content of education in the Old Testament?

Generally speaking, "the way of the Lord" refers to knowledge of and obedience to the will of God as revealed through act and word in Old Testament history. The way or will of God for humanity reflects his personal character and attributes. As human beings love their neighbors as themselves (Lev 19:18), practice righteousness and justice (Gen 18:19), and pursue holiness (Lev 11:44) they walk in the way of the Lord in that they mirror God's character. Education was essentially instruction in covenant obedience or "keeping the way of the Lord" (Gen 18:19). Moses summarized the basic components of this covenant in his farewell address to the Israelites as loving God, walking in His ways, and keeping His commandments, statutes, and ordinances (Deut 30:16). Later, the psalmist condensed this covenant content of Old Testament education into the phrase "the law of the Lord" (Psalm 119:1).

Naturally, the content of Hebrew education expanded as God continued to reveal himself and his redemptive plan to the Israelites through the centuries of Old Testament history. For example, the details of Yahweh's covenant with Abraham fills but three chapters in Genesis (12, 15, 17). By contrast, the details of the Mosaic covenant dominate the greater portions of the biblical literature found in Exodus, Leviticus, Numbers, and Deuteronomy. Since the Israelites recognized Yahweh as the God of history, providentially active during human events, history too became part of the content or curriculum of Hebrew education.

The recitation and festal remembrance of divine Acts in human history were instructive as to the nature of God and his purposes in creation. The primary example of this historical trajectory in Hebrew education is the Passover feast and exodus from Egypt (Ex.12:24-27 ; 13:11-16). In the past, the Hebrew poetic and wisdom traditions were included in the covenant content in Old Testament education. The wisdom of tradition served as a practical commentary on the law or covenant legislation, while the prophetic tradition functioned as a theological commentary on Old Testament law. Like the legal tradition associated with the covenants, both wisdom and prophecy were rooted in the behavioral outcomes of loving God and doing righteousness and justice (Proverbs 1:3 Proverbs 2:9 ; Hosea 6:6 ; Micah 6:8).The

PRACTICE OF EDUCATION

Until a child was about five years old informal education in the home was largely the responsibility of the mother, a nurse, or a male guardian. A youth between the ages of five and twenty usually worked with his father as an apprentice learning a vocation. No doubt parental instruction in the ways of the Lord continued through these years, reinforced through association with the extended family and involvement in the ritual of community worship. In later Judaism, male children between the ages of five and twenty usually attended synagogue schools and were trained in the Torah, the Mishnah, and the Talmud.

Young women were educated in the way of the Lord and in culturally acceptable domestic skills by their mothers or other women of some standing. Several professions were open to women, including those of a nurse and midwife, cook, weaver, perfumer, singer, mourner, and servant. In certain cases, women assumed prominent positions of leadership, like the prophet-judge Deborah (Judges 4:4-5) and the prophetess-sage Huldah (2 Kings 22:14-15).

It seems likely that women of royal standing in Jerusalem received formal schooling similar to that of their male counterparts since they were part of the official political system and a queen'srule was a possibility in the ancient Near Eastern world. Theologically, the practice of education as outlined in Old Testament revelation resulted in God's covenant blessing for the Hebrew. These divine blessings included political autonomy and security, as well as agricultural and economic prosperity (Lev 26:1-8). Sociologically, the practice of education facilitated assimilation into a community of faith and ensured stabilisation because the principle of "doing justice" permeated society (Leviticus 19:15 Leviticus 19:18). Religiously, the practice of education sustained a covenant relationship with God through obedience and proper ritual, which prompted God's favor and presence with Israel (Lev 26:9-12).

The Agencies or organisations established to provide of Education: There were basically three agencies or institutions responsible for the education of youth in Old Testament times: the home or family, the community, and formal centers of learning. Here it is important to remember that the process of education described in Scripture was predominantly informal (Home and community), not the formal education of learned institutions. The home was the primary agency for instruction in Hebrew society. While the Old Testament emphasizes the role of the father as teacher, both parents are given charge to train their children (Proverbs 1:8 Proverbs 6:20 ; 31:26).

Since ancient Israel was largely a clan society, extended family members like grandparents, aunts and uncles, and even cousins participated in the educational process within the home. The "home school" curriculum was both religious and vocational, as parents and other family members tutored children in "the fear of the Lord" (Prov 2:5) and a trade or professional skill,most often that of the father.

Since all Israelites were bonded together in a covenant relationship as the people of God before Yahweh, the religious community also played an important role in the education of the Hebrew. Again, community instruction was essentially religious in nature and took the form of didactic and historical meditation, moral training, sign and symbol, memorisation and catechism, festival and sacrificial liturgy, ritual enactment, and priestly role modeling. Specific examples of community education include: the three great pilgrimage festivals (Unleavened Bread, Weeks, and Tabernacles Deut 16:16 ; Exod 12:14-28), the public reading of the Mosaic law every seventh year (Deut 31:12-13), the covenant renewal enactments (Deut. 29-30; Josh. 23-24), the annual national festivals/fasts, sabbath worship, historical teaching memorials, tabernacle/temple architecture and furnishings, the sacrificial system, and priestly dress and liturgical function. Further examples are the Jerusalem temple conservatory of music (1 Chron 25:8), and the office of sage or counselor associated with Israelite kingship (1 Kings 4:5-6 ; 1 Kings 12:6 1 Kings 12:10 ; Jer 18:18).

Education in Later Judaism: Important developments in education during this period included the rise of the synagogue as both a religious and educational institution; the emergence of scribal schools for copying, studying, and interpreting the Hebrew Scriptures; and the establishment of "schools" or academies for the study of the Torah. There were lead under the tutelage of well-known rabbis or teachers. Three items deserve mention in the development of the educational process in Judaism because of their theological significance for the New Testament and Christianity.

First, the formative period of Judaism (roughly from the reforms of Ezra to the time of Maccabees) witnessed the expansion of the religious content or curriculum of Jewish education. The Mishnah, an accumulated oral tradition, supplemented the Mosaic Law. The Talmud was accorded equal standing with the Old Testament Scriptures in the Jewish rabbinic schools. In part, this led to the rift between Jesus and his religious Jewish counterparts because he rejected the authority of the oral tradition, decrying a religion that neglected the law of God to cling to the traditions of men (Mark 7:1-9).

Second, the emphasis on law keeping or obedience to God's commands eventually led to a pharisaical legalism that tithed spice seeds with ruthless calculation (Matt 23:23). Regrettably, devotion to the law of God displaced devotion to God himself so that certain circles of Judaism now ignored the very essence of Torah faith, justice, and mercy.

Third, the idea of biblical study as worship emerges during this time period. The precedent for understanding study as an act of worship stems from the Old Testament, where the psalmist remarked that all those who delight in the works of God's study will "worshipfully investigate" them (Psalm 111:2).Education in New Testament Times: The New Testament understanding of education is simply adopted from the practice of the Old Testament and Judaism. For example, the family remains the primary context for education, with prominence also given to the church as the extended community of faith. The New Testament focuses its attention on educating the whole person (Intellect, emotions, and will), education through personal relationships (i.e., the mentoring relationship of teacher and disciple), the process of both instilling knowledge and encouraging learning through discovery and educating through experiential learning. Especially important theologically is the education of the whole person (so that intellectual knowledge is applied to personal behavior James 1:25 ; 1 John 2:2-6); and the work of God's Spirit in illuminating the learner as he or she is instructed in the faith (John 16:5-15 ; 1 John 2:26-27).

THE TEACHING COMES FROM GOD

According to the Gospel records, much of Jesus' public ministry was spent teaching his disciples, as well as the crowds. Jesus was recognized and acknowledged as a teacher (or rabbi) by his disciples, the general public, and by contemporary Jewish religious leaders, including Nicodemus who identified Jesus as "a teacher who has come from God" (John 3:2). Indeed, Jesus even referred to himself as teacher on several occasions (Mark 14:14 ; John 13:13). The Gospels consistently report that people were astonished or amazed at the teaching of Jesus

(Mark 1:22 ; 11:18 ; Luke 4:32). What made Jesus a "master teacher"? Granted he was God incarnate, a unique human being as the Son of Man. And yet, the approach, method, and content utilized by Jesus in his teaching continue to be paradigmatic for Christian education. Jesus sometimes initiated the teaching moment (the Samaritan woman in John 4), but many times, the learner(s) engaged Jesus in a teaching moment (Nic. in Jn.3). Jesus also had the ability to teach effectively in informal educational settings (Mark 12:35), or more spontaneously as the need arose or circumstance dictated (Mark 9:33-37). Jesus was not afraid to hide the truth from some (those who were not seeking the truth or those who in their pride thought they already possessed it) so others could find the truth (Matt 13:10-17). Jesus also prevented Christian church(es) from being duped by "strange teachings" (Eph 4:14 ; 2 Thess 2:15). Also, the teaching of apostolic doctrine fostered both Christian discernment of false teachers, and their lies (1 Tim 1:3-7). Teaching was integral to the apostolic mission as Jesus charged his disciples to take the gospel of the kingdom of God to the nations (Matt 28:20). Early on this teaching consisted of systematic instruction in the apostles' doctrine (informally? cf. Acts 2:42), and the public reading and teaching of Scripture in corporate worship (1 Tim 4:13). Later, catechism or oral instruction in Christian doctrine became a necessary prelude to baptism in early church practice. Only through sound teaching could people come to know the truth and escape the snare of the evil one (2 Tim 2:24-26). Since teaching was vital to Christian faith, life, and growth, Christ endowed his church with spiritual gifts including the office of pastor-teacher (Eph 4:11) and the gift of teaching (Rom 12:7 ; 1 Corinthians 14:6 1 Corinthians 14:26). Teachers were distinguished as leaders in the church, along with apostles and prophets, from the earliest days of church history (cf. Acts 13:1). In addition, one of the requirements for the office of bishop or elder in the church was the ability to teach (1 Tim 3:2 ; 2 Tim 2:24 ; Titus 2:9). The basic purpose of Christian teaching according to Paul was godliness instruction leading to maturity in Christ (Col 1:28). Ultimately, biblical education is instruction in a lifestyle. For this reason, the apostle Paul reminded his pupil Timothy, "you know all about my teaching, my way of life continue in what you learned" (2 Timothy 3:10 2 Timothy 3:14). The Global Partnership for Education (GPE), a global collaboration between more than 60 developing countries, is working on the front lines to increase access to education in some places around the globe. On February 1st, 2018, GPE leaders convened in Dakar, Senegal for the third GPE replenishment, aimed at raising $3.1 billion in new investment for the fund. Global Partnership is aiming to raise $3.1 billion in a new investment from donor countries to be put into the GPE fund, as well as to increase other aid to education. GPE is asking developing country partners to pledge increases in their own domestic financing. They help developing countries to increase their own domestic financing for education, acting as a global donor in support for an education decreasing at an alarming rate. In 2016, the Global Partnership for Education helped to train 238,000 teachers worldwide.

SPIRITUAL EROSION OF NATIONAL PRIDE AND IDENTITY

Webster defines erosion as "the process of where something is diminished or destroyed by degrees".It is an assessment of successes and failures of people, together with a subjective cheerful feeling caused by belonging to a nation. This feeling is a result of appraisal, comparisons, and observations embedded in the individuals' experience, connected with their native land's destiny.

Here are some verses that will reveal that anytime a Godly servant may fall. An active spiritual leader may collapse and a strong foundation that we built for many years may collapse. (1Pe 5:8) Be self-controlled and alert. Your enemy the devil prowls around like a roaring lion looking for someone to devour. (Luk 4:13) That completed the testing, the devil retreated temporarily, lying in wait for another opportunity. (1Co 10:12) So, if you think you are standing firm, be careful that you don't fall! (1Co 9:26) Therefore I do not run like a man running aimlessly; I do not fight like a man beating the air. (1Co 9:27) No, I beat my body and make it my slave so that after I have preached to others, I myself will not be disqualified for the prize. The Unseen danger, though real, we hardly accept and recognize it. Spiritual erosion though fatal is enjoyable while still in secret from the eyes of men. Everything is laid bare to God's eyes (Heb. 4:13) even uncontrollable desire. (2 Samuel 11:1) In the spring of the year, at the time when kings normally conduct wars, David sent out Joab with his soldiers and the entire Israelite army, they defeated the Ammonites and besieged Rabbah. One evening David got up from his bed and walked around on the roof of his palace. From the roof he saw a woman bathing. Now this woman was very attractive. (2 Samuel 11:3) David sent someone to inquire about the woman. The messenger said, "Isn't this Bathsheba, the daughter of Eliam, the wife of Uriah the Hittite?" Those who are on the process of spiritual erosion do not know that they are slowly losing their sensitivity toward God.

ECONOMIC POVERTY

Poverty is the inability to reach a minimum accepted standard of living in a particular society. Poverty isa multifaceted concept, which has many branches, namely: social, economic, and political elements. Absolute poverty, extreme poverty, or destitution refers to the complete lack of the means necessary to meet basic personal needs such as food, clothing and shelter. In the New Testament, riches were associated with ostentatious displays of gold and fine clothes (James 2:17), sumptuous feasting (Luke 16:19), self-indulgence (Luke 19:16-20), stinginess toward the poor (Luke 16:19-31), fraud against workers (James 5:4), and wandering away from the faith (1 Timothy 6:9-10).

With this in mind, The New Testament appropriately condemns rich people with self-indulgent attitudes, while also encouraging the creation of wealth. Wealth is created as people obey the Lord's cultural mandate of Genesis 1:28 to subdue the world and make it useful for human beings. In the first century, this was mostly accomplished through diligent farming and honest trading (2 Timothy 2:6; Acts 18:1-3). As wealth was created, people were prepared to share with those in need (Ephesians 4:28). People were expected to view wealth as a stewardship. For example, Lydia was a wealthy merchant but was not distracted by her expensive goods from hearing the gospel message from Paul (Acts 16:14).

Another cause of poverty in the New Testament was those who became rich by oppressing the (James 5: 1-4) or by hoarding riches in the face of obvious needs (Luke 12:15-21). In the early century, creating wealth was not easy because most of the population was employed in subsistence farming. Riches were commonly accumulated through oppressing workers, exploiting slaves, and taxing people heavily. The cause of poverty resulted from laziness or moral foolishness such that an individual failed to create wealth through honest work (2 Thessalonians 3:11; Ephesians 4:28; Luke 15:11-24). Church leaders were instructed to admonish the idle (1 Thessalonians 5:14) and rebuke the lazy (Titus 1:12-13).A gain, the cause of poverty involved sudden disasters that destroyed wealth.

FACING THE GROWING UNEMPLOYMENT CHALLENGES IN AFRICA

According to an International Labour Organisation both Northern Africa and sub-Saharan Africa face risks of slowing progress in terms of jobs quality and productive opportunities. By counting (ILO) in an African context, it was found that unemployment appears to be on a downward trend in Northern Africa, but labour market distress remains pervasive, especially among women and youth. Northern Africa still exhibits the highest unemployment rate globally, at 12.1 per cent in 2015, however this is an improvement from 12.5 per cent a year earlier and marks the first decrease since 2011.

In the intervening period, growth continued to be too low and not sufficiently inclusive to make a significant impact on youth unemployment. Northern Africa has the highest regional youth unemployment rate in the world, at close to 30 per cent in 2015, with little sign that it will decline in the near future. On top of that, large shares of youth find themselves not in education, employment or training (NEET). Data shows that, among those aged 15-29, NEETs account for 32 per cent in Tunisia (reaching some 42 per cent of young women) and 40 per cent in Egypt (64 per cent of young women).

UNEMPLOYMENT IN THE BIBLE

Jeremiah 29:11-14 states "For I know the plans I have for you, declares the Lord, plans for welfare and not for evil, to give you a future and a hope. Then you will call upon me and come and pray to me, and I will hear you. You will seek me and find me, when you seek me with all your heart. I will be found by you, declares the Lord, and I will restore your fortunes and gather you from all the nations and all the places where I have driven you, declares the Lord, and I will bring you back to the place from which I sent you into exile." The situation for female labour force participation continues to be an unchanged chronic issue in northern Africa, where the female rate of employment, 22.5 per cent, is considerably lower than males at 73.8 per cent, bringing the average for both sexes to 48 per cent, the lowest of all regions in the world. The loss of employment and/or income is one of the most distressing events in life, especially for those supporting a family. Foreclosure on the family home or having to declare bankruptcy due to unemployment adds additional fear, uncertainty, and emotional turmoil.

PROMISES FOR THOSE STRUGGLING WITH UNEMPLOYMENT

How is the Christian to react to these catastrophic life events? What biblical principles can we apply to the loss of a home or a job and benefits (health/life insurance, retirement)? Promises are real, If you are unemployed, there's nothing more important than faith. In the Bible, faith means trusting all that God promises to be with us in Christ Jesus. So, if you are going to have faith, one of the most crucial steps is to understand the promises of God. Let us then with confidence draw near to the throne of grace, so that we may receive mercy and find grace to help in time of need. (Hebrews 4:16) Unemployment is not sin but all of us, employed and unemployed, have sinned. The good news is that because Jesus died to pay for our sins, if we will turn to Jesus Christ and trust Him, He will give us everything we need.

Look at God's promise in Psalm 50:15 —call upon me in the day of trouble; I will deliver you, and you shall glorify me. If you genuinely confess any wrongdoing, humble yourself before Jesus Christ, and call upon Him, He will deliver you. There may be consequences for what you've done but God won't turn from us because of sin or mistakes. Remember how Abraham's lie caused his wife Sarah to be taken into Pharaoh's harem? God had mercy on them and delivered Sarah. He will also deliver you.

God will bless you through wrongs others have done. What if you lost your job because of an unjust boss, someone's slander, or foolish politicians? It would be easy to see yourself as a victim but you are not. Even the wrongs done to you by others are part of God's plan to bring you great good. For example, Joseph's brothers sold him into slavery resulting in years in a dungeon, but look at how he describes this when he's talking to his brothers. "As for you, you meant evil against me, but God meant it for good, to bring it about that many people should be kept alive, as they are today" (Gen.50:20.)

No one can do anything to you that will cause the ultimate loss. God has planned every loss as a way to bring you a great and glorious good. God is in complete control, He is not worried about GDP growth, unemployment figures, or manufacturing indexes. He controls everything, including the heart of every business owner in your city.

The king's heart is a stream of water in the hand of the LORD; he turns it wherever he will. (Prov.21: 1) God will provide the job and income you need. That's what Jesus promises in (Matt. 6: 33), "but seek first the kingdom of God and his righteousness, and all these things will be added to you." There is the condition that we must first seek His kingdom and righteousness. That doesn't mean seeking Him perfectly this side of heaven, as none of us seeks God perfectly. Rather it means seeking Him genuinely, earnestly, and confessing when we fail. It's important to understand that God has ordained work for mankind. Work is described in the Bible as beneficial in that it provides for our needs (Prov.14:23; Eccl; 3:13, 5:18-19) and gives us the resources to share with others in need (Ephesians 4:28).

Paul reminded the believers in Thessalonica that anyone who was not willing to work should not eat (2 Thessalonians 3:10) and that he himself worked as not to be a burden on anyone (Acts 18:3; 2 Corinthians 11:9). So, loss of employment should not be an excuse for laziness, and all due diligence should be exercised to find other employment as quickly as possible (Proverbs 6:9-11).

At the same time, it may not be possible to find a position equal in pay and status to the one that was lost. In these cases, Christians should not allow pride to keep them from taking jobs in other fields, even if it means lowered status or less pay, at least temporarily.

We should also be willing to accept help from other believers and our churches, perhaps in exchange for work that needs to be done in homes, yards, and church facilities. Extending and accepting a "helping hand" in these times is a blessing to those who give and to those who receive. It exhibits the "law of Christ," which is love for one another

(Galatians 6:2). Similarly, even the loss of the family home through foreclosure or bankruptcy can be a time of blessing for the family, as it can be a time when parents and children "close ranks" and become more keenly aware of their love for one another and the important things in life. This can include faith, family and community and as well as a shift away from focus on material things that have no eternal value and can disappear in a moment.

God can also use these circumstances to remind us of the truth spoken by Jesus (Matt. 6: 19-20) and refocus our hearts on heavenly treasure. Above all, renewing our faith and trust in God's promises is of utmost importance during times of financial stress. Revisiting passages that speak of God's faithfulness to His children will strengthen and encourage us when the future looks bleak. First Corinthians 10:13 reminds us that God is faithful, will not test us beyond our ability to bear it and will provide a way out of the trial. If that's your heart, then God who has always been, who created the heavens and the earth, who has never broken a promise, swears that He will provide the job and income you need.

This is not necessarily the job and income you want but the job and the income you need in order to fulfill His call and find the greatest joy in Him. God has a perfect plan for each day you are unemployed. Since God is in complete control, each day you are unemployed is a day He has chosen to have you be unemployed. God has a meaningful activity for you during each of those days. So, what does He want you to do exactly? He will give you wisdom to answer this question (James 1:5). According to Habakkuk 3:17-18 the fig tree should not blossom, nor fruit be on the vines, the producer of the olive fail and the fields yield no food, the flock be cut off from the fold and there be no herd in the stalls, yet I will rejoice in the LORD; I will take joy in the God of my salvation. So ask God to pour His Spirit upon you. Plead with Him to free you from trusting a job for your joy. Set your heart upon Scriptures describing Him. And pray over those Scriptures until you see that Jesus is all you need. Not one word of all the good promises that the LORD had made to the house of Israel had failed; all came to pass. (Joshua 21:45)

God has a perfect track record. He fulfilled every promise He made to the house of Israel and because of Jesus' death on the Cross, and your trust in Him, He will fulfill every promise He's made to you. Poor job quality remains a pressing issue worldwide, with over 1.5 billion people in vulnerable employment, representing nearly half the global workforce. The situation is particularly endemic in Sub-Saharan Africa where over 70 per cent of workers are in vulnerable employment against the global average of 46.3 percent.

CORE CHALLENGES FOR NORTHERN AFRICA INCLUDE THE FOLLOWING

High unemployment and youth unemployment rate (SDG targets 8.5, 8 .6 and 8.8): As it stands, the youth unemployment rate in Northern Africa is the highest of all regions, reaching 45 per cent for female youth. Addressing this challenge is of particular importance, as high rates of unemployment have been linked to political instability in the region.

The coverage of social protection systems including social assistance is uneven and fragmented in the Northern Africa region. Pension coverage varies across the region, reaching 30–40 per cent of the workforce in countries such as Algeria, Egypt, Morocco and Tunisia, but reaching a very small proportion of the population in countries such as Sudan. Furthermore, informal workers are not covered by any social protection scheme.

CORE CHALLENGES FOR SUB-SAHARAN AFRICA INCLUDE THE FOLLOWING

Decent work (SDG target 8.5): Despite relatively low unemployment rates and high labour force participation, underemployment, working poverty and poor job quality remain significant problems. ILO labour standards: Ratification of the ILO fundamental conventions is high in the region: six countries have not ratified the eight fundamental principles. However, countries in the region lack sufficient institutional capacity for enforcement evidenced by the widespread breaches of the core standards (SDG target 8.8). Social dialogue and collective bargaining: Effective social dialogue is necessary for inclusive and sustainable growth. While data is not sufficient to comprehensively evaluate the status of social dialogue and collective bargaining in the region, trade union density in general is low (generally below 5 per cent; highest in South Africa at 24.9 per cent (2008)). Collective bargaining coverage is generally at 10 per cent or less of total employment (SDG 9).

URBAN GROWTH AND URBANISATION

Urban is derived from the Latin 'Urbs' a term used by the Romans to refer to a city. Urban sociology is the sociology of urban living for groups and the social relationships in urban environments. Thompson Warren has defined it as the movement of people from communities concerned solely with agriculture to other communities, generally larger, whose activities are primarily centered in government, trade, manufacture or allied interests. Urbanisation is a two-way process because it involves not only movement from villages to cities and change from agricultural occupations to business, trade, service and profession, but it also involves change in the migrants' attitudes, beliefs, values and behavior patterns. Urbanisation is the movement of population from rural to urban areas and the resulting increasing proportion of a population that resides in urban rather than rural places. There is a rapid migration of rural people to urban areas for jobs and better living. As a result, the populations in towns are increasing and rural population is dwindling. The rapid in rush of people to the urban areas is putting pressure on its limited space and causes all types of health and environmental hazards.

ADVANTAGES OF URBANISATION

Growth in industrial productions: The production in various industrial sectors like cement, iron and steel, textile, fertilizers and computing help the economic growth of the country. Export increases and forest reserve increases.

Growth in trade and commerce: Urbanisation helps the nation's business sector. Rural people came to urban places with their goods. People from foreign countries are attracted to goods in cities, and towns gain better transport facilities. Tourism is a good source of foreign currency for a country.

DISADVANTAGES OF URBANISATION

The decrease in the rural population effects agricultural production due to shortage of workers in rural areas. The increases in population in urban places place pressure on water and sanitation facilities. It results in environmental pollution and health hazards. The unemployment rate increases in urban areas due to the various criminal activities that impact law and order.

Land use in North America is defined in terms of individual ownership rights. Much of current thinking about land use and property rights has been shaped by the seventeenth century philosopher John Locke. Locke claimed that ownership of property is the most important of three inherent God-given rights, the other two rights being the right to life and the right to liberty (Long Jr., 49). Only now are we seeing the fallacy in this statement. The design of the Levites' urban settlements featured open spaces and regional integration. Then comes the ill-fated city of Babel, with its problematic urban architecture, followed by the original sin-cities, Sodom and Gomorrah. The only apparent exception to this inclination is the sanctity Jerusalem, the city of God.

Besides, if there's one social-environmental issue that seems uniquely modern it is the phenomenal growth of urbanisation. As recently as 1800, only 2.5% of humankind (20 million people) lived in cities, and there were only nine cities with populations of over a million. By 1900 that swelled to 10% (160 million), and 27 megalopolises. Now, more than half the world's population, over 3 billion live in cities, with at least 240 cities of a million inhabitants or more.

Levitical Cities Surrounded by Green Space: At the end of the book of Numbers, the Israelites are still wandering in the wilderness and there is already talk of the boundaries and tribal shares in the Land. The greatest tribes received large areas to afford extensive agriculture and animal husbandry. One tribe remained essentially landless, relegated to urban areas: the tribe of Levi. The Levites and their work in the Temple are supported by tithes, and therefore they receive no nachalah, no "territorial share" among the tribes (cf. Numbers 18:23-24). No large farms perhaps, but this week's portion (Ch. 35) requires setting aside no less than 48 Levitical cities and includes instructions for their layout.

Biblical views on urban and regional planning are a key component of this plan is the prohibition of rezoning. According to the Sabbatical and Jubilee Laws (13:4-5), based on the (Babylonian) (Arachin 33b) rules, it is forbidden to build in these open spaces, to expand the city at the expense of pastureland or fields. Moreover, he states categorically that Levitical cities are not a special case: this applies equally to all other cities in Israel.

Rabbi Samson Raphael Hirsch (1808-1888), founder and prime

expositor of modern Orthodoxy, living in a time of great urban expansion, commented on this ruling and wrote with great fervor regardingthe responsibility of one generation to another concerning the land. On Leviticus 25:34, stating that a Levitical city and surrounding area "is a possession unto them forever", he writes: "Precisely because the city with its open spaces has been given to them for all the succeeding generations, no generation is permitted to change it as it sees fit. The present generation is not the sole ruler over it, but the future generations are equal in their rights."

A century after Hirsch, the influential contemporary urban historian and theoretician, Lewis Mumford wrote extensively of the importance of the regional setting of the city. "The hope of the city," he argued, "lies outside itself." The minimal unit of urban living is much larger than the built area: a city can't be built, conceived, or occupied apart from its ecological region. Mumford echoes Hirsch's endorsement of synthesis in his support of attempts to "build up a more exhilarating kind of environment—not as a temporary haven of refuge but as a permanent seat of life and culture, urban in its advantages, permanently rural in its situation."God, the Creator of all things, rules over all and deserves our worship/adoration (Ps.103:19-22). The earth, and with it all the cosmos, reveals its Creator's wisdom and goodness (Ps. 19:1—6) is sustained and governed by His power and loving-kindness (Ps. 102:25—27; Ps. 104; Col. 1:17; Heb. 1:3, 10—12).

Men and women were created in the image of God, given a privileged place among creatures, and commanded to exercise stewardship over the earth (Gen. 1:26—28; Ps. 8:5). Fundamental to a properly Christian environmental ethic then, is the Creator/creature distinction and the doctrine of humankind's creation in the image of God. Some environmentalists, especially those in the "Deep Ecology" movement, divinize the earth and insist on "biological egalitarianism,". This is the equal value and rights of all life forms, in the mistaken notion that this will raise human respect for the earth. Instead, this philosophy negates the biblical affirmation of the human person's unique role as steward and eliminates the very rationale for human care for creation. The quest for the humane treatment of beasts by lowering people to the level of animals leads only to the beastly treatment of humans.

The image of God consists of knowledge and righteousness, expressing itself in creative human stewardship and dominion over the earth (Gen. 1:26—28; 2:8—20; 9:6; Eph. 4:24).Our stewardship under God implies that we are morally accountable to him for treating creation in a manner that best serves the objectives of the kingdom of God. However both moral accountability and dominion over the earth depend on the freedom to choose. The exercise of these virtues and this calling requires that we act in an arena of considerable freedom – not unrestricted license - but freedom exercised within the boundaries of God's moral law, revealed in Scripture and in the human conscience (Exod. 20:1—17; Deut. 5:6—21; Rom. 2:14—15). These facts are not vitiated by the fact that humankind fell into sin (Gen. 3). Rather, our sinfulness has brought God's responses. Firstly judgment, subjecting humankind to death and separation from God (Gen. 2:17; 3:22—24; Rom. 5:12—14; 6:23) and subjecting creation to the curse of futility and corruption (Gen. 3:17—19; Rom. 8:20—21). Then in restoration, through Christ's atoning, redeeming death for his people, reconciling them to God (Rom. 5:10—11, 15—21; 2 Cor. 5:17—21; Eph. 2:14—17; Col. 1:19—22), and through his wider work of delivering the earthly creation from its bondage to corruption (Rom. 8:19—23). Indeed, Christ even involves fallen humans in this work of restoring creation (Rom. 8:21).

As Francis Bacon put it in Novum Organum Scientiarum (New Method of Science), "Man by the fall fell at the same time from his state of innocence and from his dominion over creation. Both of these losses, however, can even in this life be in some parts repaired, the former by religion and faith, the latter by the arts and sciences."[d] Sin makes it difficult for humans to exercise godly stewardship, but the work of Christ makes it possible nonetheless.

When he created the world, God set aside a unique place called the Garden of Eden, and placed in it the first man, Adam (Gen. 2:8—15). God instructed Adam to cultivate and guard the Garden (Gen. 2:15)– to enhance its already great fruitfulness and to protect it against the encroachment of the surrounding wilderness that made up the rest of the earth. Having also created the first woman and having joined her to Adam (Gen. 2:18—25), God commanded them and their descendants to multiply, to spread out beyond the boundaries of the Garden of Eden, and to fill, subdue, and rule the whole earth and everything in it (Gen. 1:26, 28). Both by endowing them with his image and by placing them in authority over the earth, God gave men and women superiority and priority over all other earthly creatures. This implies that proper environmental stewardship, while it seeks to harmonize the fulfillment of the needs of all creatures, nonetheless puts human needs above non-human needs when the two are in conflict.

Some environmentalists reject this vision as "anthropocentric" or "specialist," and instead promote a "biocentric" alternative. The alternative, however, attractively humble it might sound, is untenable. People, alone among creatures on earth, have both the rationality and the moral capacity to exercise stewardship, to be accountable for their choices, to take responsibility for caring not only for themselves but also for other creatures. To reject human stewardship is to embrace, by default, no stewardship. The only proper alternative to selfish anthropocentrism is not biocentrism but ethnocentrism. This refers to a vision of earthly care with God and his perfect moral law at the centre, as human beings act as His accountable stewards.

Two groups of interrelated conditions are necessary for responsible stewardship. One group are conditions related to the freedom that allows people to use and exchange the fruits of their labor for mutual benefit (Matt. 20:13—15). These conditions–knowledge, righteousness, and dominion–provide an arena for the working out of the image of God in the human person. In another group are conditions related to responsibility, especially to the existence of a legal framework that holds people accountable for harm they may cause to others (Rom. 13:1—7; Exod. 21:28—36; 22:5—6). These two sets of conditions provide the safeguards necessitated by human sinfulness. Both sets are essential to responsible stewardship; neither may be permitted to crowd out the other, and each must be understood in light of both the image of God and the sinfulness of man. Freedom, an expression of the image of God, may be abused by sin and therefore, needs restrictions (1 Pet. 2:16). Governmental power, a power necessary to subdue sin and reduce its harm, may be exercised by sinful humans, who may also abuse it (Ps. 94:20; 1 Sam. 8). This means that it, too, needs restrictions (Acts 4:19—20; 5:29). Such restrictions are reflected not only in specific limits on governmental powers (Deut. 17:14—20), but also in the division of powers into judicial, legislative, and executive (reflecting God as the Judge, Lawgiver, and King) (Isa. 33:22). This encompasses the separation of powers into local and central. This concept is exemplified in the distinct rulers of the tribes of Israel and the prophets or kings Israel [Deut. 1:15—16], the gradation of powers from lesser to greater (Exod. 18; Deut. 16:8—11), and the vesting of power in a people to elect their rulers (Deut. 1:9—15; 17:15). These principles are reflected in the Constitution of the United States. Also crucial to the Christian understanding of government is the fact that God has ordained governments to do justice by punishing those who do wrong and praise those who do right (Rom. 13:1—4; 1 Pet. 2:13—14).

These principles indicate that a biblically sound environmental stewardship is fully compatible with private-property rights and a free economy, if people are held accountable for their actions. Stewardship can best be accomplished, we believe, by a carefully limited government (in which collective action takes place at the most local level possible to minimize the breadth of harm done in case of government failure) and through a rigorous commitment to virtuous human action in the marketplace and in government.

These principles, when applied, promote both economic growth and environmental quality. On the one hand, there is a direct and positive correlation between the degree of political and economic freedom with both the level of economic attainment and the rapidity of economic growth in countries around the world. The 20 percent of the world's countries with the greatest economic freedom produce, on average, over ten times as much wealth per capita as the 20 percent with the least economic freedom. While the freest countries enjoyed an average 2.27 percent annual rate of growth in real gross national product per capita through the 1990s, the least-free countries experienced a decline of 1.32 percent per year. On the other hand, there is also a direct and positive correlation between economic advances and environmental quality. The freer, wealthier countries have experienced consistent reductions in pollution/improvements in their environment, while the less free, poorer countries have experienced either increasing environmental degradation or much slower environmental improvement. We shall return to this correlation shortly. First, however, it behoves us to know something of the changes in our material condition over the last few centuries.

Prior to 250 years ago, everywhere in the world, the death rate was so close to the birth rate that population grew only about 0.17 percent per year, doubling approximately every 425 years, instead of every forty-two years at the world's average growth rate in the 1980s, or every fifty-one years at the average rate for the 1990s. Infant and child mortality rates (around 40 percent overall) were little better for the very rich royalty than they were for farmers and peasants, even into the eighteenth century. Britain's Queen Anne (1665—1714), for instance, was pregnant eighteen times; five of her children survived birth; none survived childhood. Eighteenth-century French farming – the best in Europe – produced only about 345 pounds of wheat per acre; modern American farmers produce 2,150 pounds per acre, about 6.2 times as much. Early-fifteenth-century French farmers produced about 2.75 to 3.7 pounds of wheat per man-hour, and the rate fell by about half over the next two centuries.[14] Modern American farmers produce about 857 pounds per man-hour[15]—about 230 to 310 times as much as their French counterparts in the 1400s, and 460 to 620 times as much as French farmers around 1600. (This means that modern farmers also manage to farm from 37 to 100 times as many acres, thanks largely to mechanized equipment and advanced farming techniques.) As the great French historian Fernand Braudel pointed out; it became very difficult to sustain life when productivity in wheat fell below 2.2 pounds per man-hour.

For most of the 350 years from 1540 to 1890, productivity in France (which, as was fairly typical of Western Europe, suffered a serious decline in productivity at the start of that period) was well below that.[16] Such facts help to explain why earlier generations spent a major part of each day working to earn enough income just to pay for food while we spend far less on food today (Under 6 percent of total consumer expenditures in the United States in the 1980s went to food). These developments – along with the advent of glass window treatment of drinking water and sewage, mechanical refrigeration, adoption of safer methods of work, travel, and recreation, sanitary medical practices, antibiotics and modern surgical techniques – also help to explain why people live about three times as long now. While "man is destined to die once" (Heb. 9:27), the Bible recognizes death as punishment for sin and, consequently, as man's enemy (1 Cor. 15:26). Long life is associated with the blessing of God (Exod. 20:12; Deut. 11:8—9; Eph. 6:1—3) and with the reign of the Messiah (Isa. 65:20). Economic development is a good to be sought, not as an end, but as a means toward genuine human benefit. For instance, consider a few of the things absolutely no one – not even royalty – could enjoy before the last two centuries of economic advance: Electricity and all that it powers. This includes lights, telephones, radios, televisions, refrigerators, air conditioners, fans, video cassette recorders, x-rays, MRIs, computers, the Internet, high-speed printing presses, and all industrial automation. Internal combustion engines and all that they power are also included in this such as: cars, trucks, planes, farm and construction equipment, and most trains and ships.

Hundreds of synthetic materials such as plastic, nylon, orlon, rayon, vinyl, and the thousands of Products–from grocery bags would not be possible without technological advances. Before the Reformation, few countries had widespread education, and even afterward, schooling was only available principally to the rich. Two major exceptions were Germany and Scotland. In Germany, Martin Luther insisted that widespread schooling was important so that people could read the Scripture, which he had translated into the vernacular, for themselves. Similarly, in Scotland, John Knox's followers, were convinced that personal knowledge of God and his Word was essential to the maintenance of civil as well as religious liberty (Ps. 119:45; Isa. 61:1; Jer. 34:15; Luke 4:18; 2 Cor. 3:17; Gal. 5:1,13; James 1:25.)

SUPERSTITIOUS BELIEFS

Superstition is based on the ignorant faith of an object having magical powers. Another word for superstition is "idolatry." The Bible does not support the idea of things occurring by chance, but nothing is done outside of God's sovereign control. Either He causes or allows everything in keeping with His divine plan (Acts 4:28; Ephesians 1:10).

There are many types of superstitions in the world, ranging from the benign, such as not walking under a ladder, to the occult practices of astrology, black magic, divination, voodoo and sorcery. Scripture condemns those who practice astrology (Deuteronomy 4:19), magic, divination and sorcery (2 Kings 21:6, Isaiah 2:6). Idolatry is also forbidden, and no one who practices it will enter the Kingdom of God (Revelation 21:27). These types of practices are extremely dangerous because they open the minds of the practitioners to the influence of the devil. First Peter 5:8 warns us to "be self-controlled and alert. Your enemy the devil prowls around like a roaring lion looking for someone to devour."

We should get our faith not from objects or rituals of man-made origin, but from the one true God who gives eternal life. "See to it that no one takes you captive through hollow/deceptive philosophy, which depends on human tradition and the basic principles of this world rather than on Christ. For in Christ all the fullness of the Deity lives in bodily form, and you have been given fullness in Christ, who is the head over every power and authority" (Col. 2:8-10). For instance, the Jewish Law includes sacrifice and certain rituals, and promises blessing in return. There is a middle step. The burning of a calf does not directly impact the growing season; but it is obedience to God, and God promised that if the Israelites obeyed Him, He would bless them (Deut. 28:1-2). Demons, on the other hand, are attracted to those who want to see them, but all their actions toward us are malevolent. The difference, then, is if there really is a power that appreciates the action and can act correspondingly.

In 1 Kings 18:20-40, Elijah went to great lengths to show the foolishness of superstitious beliefs. He challenged the priests of Baal to a showdown, their god against The God of Israel. When their non-existent god failed to act, Elijah even taunted them—"Call out with a loud voice, for he is a god; either he is occupied or gone aside, or is on a journey, or perhaps he is asleep and needs to be awakened" (Kings 18:27). God did act (1 Kings 18:38), showing the Israelites how foolish they were for their superstitious beliefs. Paul while teaching on Mars Hill, pointed out a monument to "an unknown god." Years before, the people had been saved from calamity by a god they did not know and built the altar in thanks. The Greeks and Romans had so many gods that they set aside a place to worship the ones they hadn't even discovered yet, in hopes that fortune would come their way and disaster would be averted.

Many places globally still hold some superstitions beyond the garden variety horseshoes and broken mirrors. None of the islands of Hawaii have a completely paved road as ringing the island to do so would be to block the Menehune from being able to come and go as they wish. Feng shui, the Chinese art of arranging living spaces according to mystical energy levels, is a big business. Email chain mail that promises good fortune if forwarded to ten friends is ubiquitous.

Scientifically, superstitions fail on several levels, if an action and a result have absolutely no connection, then performing the action cannot bring about the result. Biblically, if the action is calling on a deity, force, or power that doesn't exist or doesn't have the ability to respond, then the action cannot bring about the result. If the action is done in hopes that God will act, then it had better be an action God approves of, performed with a humble, submissive attitude. Have nothing to do with godless myths and old wives' tales; rather, train yourself to be godly. 1 Timothy 4:6-7 If you point these things out to the brothers and sisters, you will be a good minister of Christ Jesus, nourished on the truths of the faith.

GENDER DISCRIMINATION

Discrimination or racism is a global issue, and some base support of it on misapplied Scripture. For example, some used a scripture that pronounces a curse against one of Noah's offspring to support the enslavement of black people several hundred years ago.

In Genesis 9:25 we read, "Cursed be Canaan. Let him become the lowest slave to his brothers carefully." It says nothing about skin color. The curse was because Ham's son, Canaan, had evidently performed some shocking act deserving of a curse. Who exactly were Canaan's descendants? Not black people, but lighter-skinned people living to the east of the Mediterranean Sea. Due to their weak practices, demonist rites, idolatry, and child sacrifices, they came under divine judgment and were known as Canaanites. The darker skinned people of Africa descended from another of Noah's offspring, Cush, who had no curse upon him. The Bible shows how God feels about people of different races in Acts 10:34, 35: "God is not partial, but in every nation the man that fears him and works righteousness is acceptable every nation the man that fears him and works righteousness is acceptable to God obedience to him is what is important, not the colour of one's skin, race, social standing, sex, or other factor. John 3:16: God loved the world so much that he gave his only begotten Son, in order that everyone exercising faith in him might not be destroyed but have everlasting life."

Gender discrimination is the belief that one gender is superior to the other, that men are superior to women. The Bible Is Crystal Clear on Gender Equality. The Bible states that in the very beginning of the human race God created man in His own image, in the image of God He created him; male and female He created them. God blessed them and said to them, "Be fruitful and increase in number; fill the earth and subdue it." (Genesis 1:27-28) In other words, the Biblical record is clear: God created men and women equal. Period. Dominion over everything was given to the woman as well as to the man. The woman was not created as inferior to the man; nor was the man greater than the woman. However, when sin entered the human race, one of the consequences was that men and women became separated from God. That basic broken relationship distorted the Divine order in many ways, one of which was that men began to rule over women (Genesis 3:16). A vast variety of religions have been established in a vein attempt to reach God, to bridge the gap between God and man that sin opened. The attempts have been futile, because man has remained a sinner, separated from God. This sinful state has been very evident in the way women have been treated throughout human history by various religions. The implied message seemed to be clear: Women are second-class citizens, objects of scorn or sex or service. Religion down through the ages has been hard on women in general. From ancient times when their babies were sacrificed to the gods, to Greek times when they were used as prostitutes in the temples, and to a lesser degree, in modern day practices where women are discriminated against or oppressed. Generally speaking, they have not been highly valued in religious circles nor in the cultures those religions influence until Jesus came. God Himself elevated the status of women forever when He chose to send His own Son, Jesus Christ, to be born of a virgin. The words and actions of Jesus underscored His elevated opinion of women, as did the early church that was established in His name following His return to heaven. His first miracle was performed in response to a plea from His mother (John 2:1-11). His first revelation of Himself as Messiah was to a woman (John 4:25- 26). His greatest miracle was performed at the request of two women (John 11:1-44). His death was memorialized by a woman (Jn.12:1-8). Women were included in His expanded group of disciples (Mark 15:41). Women stayed with Him throughout His crucifixion, even after the men had left (Matthew 27:55-56). Women observed His burial (Matthew 27:61). Following His resurrection, He appeared first to a woman (John 20:1- 16). He commissioned women as the very first evangelists (Matthew 28:1- 10; John 20:17). Women were included in the group of disciples who met daily for prayer after the ascension of Jesus (Acts 1:14). Ancient prophecy was fulfilled when the Spirit of God was given equally to men and women at Pentecost (Acts 2:17). Women were among the very first "believers" or "Christians" who made up the early church (Acts 5:14; Acts 8:12; 17:4, 12). The first church in Europe was begun with a group of women and met in the home of a woman (Acts 16:13-15). The early church was staffed by many women (Romans 16:12, Philippians 4:3). At least one early church was co-led by a woman (1 Corinthians 16:19). The very fact that the Bible goes out of its way to carefully record all the above reveals the intentionality of God's purpose to reestablish the position of women to that of equality with men. His Son, Jesus Christ, not only bridged the gap between God and man through His death on the Cross that made atonement for man's sin, He removed all barriers including that of gender, race, and nationality. This was confirmed by the apostle Paul when he stated, "There is neither Jew nor Greek, slave nor free, male nor female, for you are all one in Christ Jesus. If you belong to Christ, then you are heirs according to the promise" (Galatians 3:28-29). The discrimination that women bump into does not come from the heart of God. He created them in His own image with a capacity to know Him in a personal relationship. Today, when the Bible, which is God's Word, is read, applied, obeyed, and lived out, women are treated with respect and honor as co-heirs with Jesus Christ in the Kingdom of God (1 Peter 3:7). In summary, women may not have fared well in the world's religions, but they are greatly loved by God who, in the beginning, He created them equal to men. He created them with a capacity to know Him. When sin destroyed the relationship between men, women and Himself, God redeemed them through the death of His own Son. One day, He will welcome every woman into His heavenly home who has claimed Jesus Christ as her personal Savior and Lord. The equality, respect, and status she has longed for will reign.

CASTE DISCRIMINATION

What is caste discrimination? Caste systems are traditional, hereditary systems of social stratification, such as clans, gents, or the Indian caste system. The word caste is derived from the Portuguese word casta, meaning "lineage." Caste discrimination as the word says is discrimination of people on the basis of their caste. In ancient times the society was known to be divided into four categories namely:1. Brahamins. 2. Kshatiyas 3. Vaishyas 4. Shudras.

The four divisions of society work together as one body. The scriptures figuratively describe the body of society with the head being the brahmanas (the intellectual class), the arms being the kshatriyas (the administrative class), the stomach being the vaishyas (the agricultural class), and the legs being the shudras (the worker class). The caste system was brought to India over two thousand years ago by the invading Aryans from what is now called Iran. The Aryans were a warrior tribe who were originally nomadic, who had no skills or tradesmen in their tribe.

Alexis Charles Henri Clérel de Tocqueville (1805-1859) was one of the greatest political thinkers, most prescient commentators on American society, noted that the English in India behaved as if they too were members of a caste. According to Guy Sorman, the doctrine of caste was not specific to India but universal. Claude Alvares has written that "the English establishment themselves as a separate ruling caste, like other Indian castes, they did not inter-marry or eat with the lower class(native) caste. Their children were shipped off to public schools in England, while they themselves kept to their clubs and bungalows in special suburbs known as cantonments and civil lines."

The caste system could not have been part of Hindu religious philosophy, since it violates fundamental Hindu doctrine, according to which there is no absolute distinction between individuals, since the atman dwells in the hearts of all beings. There is no religious sanction whatsoever to the concept of the caste system in Hinduism. Alain Danielou has said: "That abusive caste practices were introduced when the administrative power ceased to be in Hindu hands, thus making the repression of abuses legally impossible."

HEALTH AND SAFETY

The Bible addresses health and safety. It's a shame when we see churches get prosecuted for health and safety breaches. A good foundation for health and safety in the New Testament is love worked no ill to his neighbour" (Romans 13: 10)

BIBLICAL HEALTH PRINCIPLES

The Bible rates health right near the top of the list in importance (3 John 1:2). Man's mind, and spiritual nature, and body are all interrelated and interdependent. God gave health rules because He knows what is best for the body (Deuteronomy 6:24, Exodus 23:25). A bondservant of Christ should eat and drink all to the glory of God - using only "that which is good" (Isaiah 55:2, 1Corinthians 10:31). If God says something is not fit to eat, He must have a good reason. He is not a harsh dictator, but a loving Father. All His counsel is for our good, always. So, if God withholds a thing from us, it is because it is not a good thing for us (Psalm 84:11). The diet God gave people at the beginning of Creation was fruit, vegetables, grains, nuts, and seeds (Genesis 1:29, 2:16; 3:18).

According to scripture the following items are unclean and forbidden: All land animals which do not have a split hoof and chew the cud (Deu.14:6); all fish and water creatures that do not have both fins and scales (Deuteronomy 14:9); all birds of prey, carrion eaters, and fish eaters (Leviticus 11:13-19), and most "creeping things" (or invertebrates) are also unclean (Leviticus 11:21-23, 41-43). If a clean food touches any unclean food, the clean food must not be eaten (Leviticus 7:19, Haggai 2:12-13).

The Bible clearly forbids the use of alcoholic beverages to induce drunkenness (Lev.10:9, Deuteronomy 21:10; 29:19, 1Samuel 1:14, 1Kings 16:9-10, Psalm 69:2, Proverbs 20:1; 21:17; 23:20-21,29-35; 26:9; 31:4-7, Isaiah 5:11-12,22; 19:14; 24:9,11; 28:1,3,7; 56:12, Jeremiah 25:27, Ezekiel 44:21, Hosea 4:11; 7:5,14, Joel 1:5; 3:3, Amos 2:8,12, Micah 2:11, Nahum 1:10, Habakkuk 2:5,15-16, Matthew 24:49, Luke 12:45; 21:34, Romans 13:13, 1Corinthians 5:11; 6:9-10, Galatians 5:19-21, Ephesians 5:18, 1 Thes.5:7, 1 Peter 4:7). Strong drink, by itself, is not unclean. God himself gave His approval of strong drink (Deu.14:26), and therefore cannot be evil in itself. At a marriage feast, Jesus worked the miracle of changing water into wine (John 2:1-11), which He would not have done if it was sinful to drink wine. Drunkenness is condemned, not wine. Some of the simple, yet very important, health laws found in the Bible are to: Eat your meals at regular intervals (Ecclesiastes 10:17), don't overeat (Proverbs 23:2, Luke 21:34), Make mealtime a happy time (Ecclesiastes 3:13). Don't harbor envy or hold grudges (Proverbs 14:30, Matthew 5:23, 24), maintain a cheerful, happy disposition (Proverbs 17:22; 23:7). Balance work and exercise with sleep and rest (Exodus 20:9,10, Ecclesiastes 2:22,23; 5:12, Psalm 127:2). Keep your body clean (Isaiah 52:11), be temperate in all things (1 Corinthians 9:25, Philippians 4:5). Avoid all harmful stimulants as medical science has confirmed the fact that tea, coffee, and soft drinks that contain the addictive drug caffeine and other harmful ingredients are all positively damaging to the body. Help those who are in need (Isaiah 58:6-8). Bury body waste to avoid disease (Deuteronomy 23:12-13, avoid eating animals that were strangled (Acts 15:20,29; 21:25), avoid eating animals that die by themselves (Leviticus 17:15; 22:8, Deuteronomy 14:21, Ezekiel 4:14). Do not boil a young animal in its mother's milk (Deuteronomy 14:21), do not eat animal fat or blood (Genesis 9:4, Leviticus 3:17; 7:23-27; 17:10-14, Deuteronomy 12:16). Recent scientific studies have confirmed the fact that most heart attacks result from a high cholesterol level in the blood -and that the use of "fats" is largely responsible for this high level. Those who break God's rules regarding the care of the body will reap broken bodies and burned-out lives (Galatians 6:7), just as one who abuses his automobile will have serious car related trouble. Those who continue to break God's laws of health will ultimately be destroyed by the Lord (1 Corinthians 3:16-17). God's health laws are not arbitrary. They are natural, established laws of the universe, like the law of gravity. Ignoring these laws always brings disastrous results. Nothing defiling or unclean will be permitted in God's kingdom (Revelation 21:27, Ezekiel 11:21). The use of improper foods defiles a man (Daniel 1:8). Choosing their "own ways" and that in which God "Delighted not" shall be slain by the Lord (Isaiah 66:3-4).

Sincere bondservants of Christ will bring their lives into harmony with God's rules, because they love Him (2 Corinthians 7:1, 1 John 3:3, John 14:15). God's counsel and rules are always for our good, just as good parents' rules and counsel are best for their children. God holds us accountable (James 4:17). The reason for restricting our diet is because we are the holy children of God (Deuteronomy 14:1-3). Take all these habits to Christ and lay them at His feet. He will joyfully give you a new heart and the power you need to break any evil habit and become a child of God (Eze.11:18,19). How thrilling and heartwarming it is to know that "with God all things are possible" (Mark 10:27). Jesus says, "Him that cometh to me I will in no wise cast out" (John 6:37). Jesus is ready to break the shackles that bind us (John 1:12). He longs to set us free, and will, if only we will permit it. Our worries, evil habits, nervous tensions, and fears will be gone when we do His bidding (Philippians 4:13). He says, "These things have I spoken unto you that your joy might be full" (Jn.15:11). The devil says freedom is found in disobedience, but this is a falsehood (John 8:44).

Paul was writing to followers of Christ whose sole "Scripture" was what we term the Old Testament! His teaching to the Corinthian Church was founded on the writings of the Old Testament. They were thoroughly familiar with the division of food into "clean and unclean." Cling to the truths that you have learned and of which you are convinced, knowing who your teachers were, and that from infancy you have known the sacred writings which are able to make you wise unto salvation.

RELIGION IN THE BIBLE

Religion is a collection of cultural systems, beliefs and world views that establishes symbols that relate humanity to spirituality and, sometimes to moral values. A critique of Geertz's model by Talal Asad categorized religion as "an anthropological category." Millions of people around the globe consider the Bible an authoritative guidebook on how to live a godly, righteous life.

"They have zeal for God, but not according to accurate knowledge. For because of not knowing the righteousness of God but seeking to establish their own, they did not subject themselves to the righteousness of God." (Romans 10:2, 3). There is only one way to heaven, and that is through Jesus Christ. There are drastic and irreconcilable differences between Christianity and all other belief systems. Every other religion is based on people doing things through their struggling while striving to earn the good favor of God.

True religion teaches the truth that is based on the Bible, not on human philosophies (John 4:24; 17:17). This includes religious truth about the soul and the hope of everlasting life on a paradise earth. (Psalm 37:29; Isaiah 35:5, 6; Ezekiel 18:4) It also does not hold back from exposing religious falsehood.—Matthew 15:9; 23:27, 28. True religion helps people to know God, including teaching them His name, Jehovah. (Psalm 83:18) . It does not teach that He is incomprehensible or aloof; rather, it teaches that He wants us to have a relationship with Him —James 4:8. True religion highlights Jesus Christ as the one through whom God grants salvation. (Acts 4:10, 12) Its members obey Jesus' commands and strive to follow his example (John 13:15; 15:14). True religion focuses on God's Kingdom as mankind's only hope (John 13:35). It teaches respect for all ethnic groups and welcomes people from all races, cultures, languages, and backgrounds. (Acts 10:34, 35) Moved by love, its members do not go to war. (Micah 4:3); True religion has no paid clergy, and it does not give high-sounding religious titles to any of its members. True religion is completely neutral in political affairs. (John 17:16; 18:36) However, its members respect and obey the government where they live, in harmony with the Bible's command: "Pay back Caesar's."

JESUS CRITICIZES THE RELIGIOUS LEADERS

Globalisation and religion as a global force - Globalisation is the increasing interconnectedness of societies, so that what happens in one locality is shaped by distant events and vice versa. It may also be referred to as the global village.

The sociology of globalisation is a subfield within sociology that deals with understanding the structures, institutions and relationships, ideologies, trends, and patterns that are particular to a globalized world. Then Jesus said to the crowds and to his disciples," The teachers of religious law and the Pharisees are the official interpreters of the Law of Moses. So, practice and obey whatever they tell you, but don't follow their example.

"Everything they do is for show. On their arms they wear extra wide prayer boxes with Scripture verses inside, and they wear robes with extra long tassels. And they love to sit at the head table at banquets and in the seats of honor in the synagogues. They love to receive respectful greetings as they walk in the marketplaces, and to be called 'Rabbi.'"

"Don't let anyone call you 'Rabbi,' for you have only one teacher, and all of you are equal as brothers and sisters. Don't address anyone here on earth as 'Father,' for only God in heaven is your Father. And don't let anyone call you 'Teacher,' for you have only one teacher, the Messiah. The greatest among you must be a servant. But those who exalt themselves will be humbled, and those who humble themselves will be exalted."

"What sorrow awaits you teachers of religious law and you Pharisees? Hypocrites! For you shut the door of the Kingdom of Heaven in people's faces. You won't go in yourselves, and you don't let others enter either. "What sorrow awaits you teachers of religious law and you Pharisees? Hypocrites! For you cross land and sea to make one convert, and then you turn that person into twice the child. "Blind guides! What sorrow awaits you!"

"For you say that it means nothing to swear 'by God's Temple,' but that it is binding to swear 'By the gold in the Temple.' Blind fools! which is more important the gold or the Temple that makes the gold sacred? You say that to swear 'by the altar' is not binding, but to swear 'by the gifts on the altar' is binding. How blind! For which is more important the gift on the altar or the altar that makes the gift sacred?"

"When you swear 'by the altar,' you are swearing by it and by everything on it. And when you swear 'by the Temple,' you are swearing by it and by God, who lives in it. And when you swear 'By heaven,' you are swearing by the throne of God and by God, who sits on the throne." "What sorrow awaits you teachers of religious law and you Pharisees? Hypocrites! For you are careful to tithe even the tiniest income from your herb gardens, but you ignore the more important aspects of the law justice, mercy, and faith.

You should tithe, yes, but do not neglect the more important things. Blind guides! You strain your water so you won't accidentally swallow a gnat, but you swallow a camel!"

"What sorrow awaits you teachers of religious law and you Pharisees? Hypocrites! For you are so careful to clean the outside of the cup and the dish, but inside you are filthy full of greed/ self-indulgence! You blind Pharisee! First wash the inside of the cup and the dish, and then the outside will become clean, too."

"What sorrow awaits you teachers of religious law and you Pharisees? Hypocrites! For you are like whitewashed tombs beautiful on the outside but filled on the inside with dead people's bones and all sorts of impurity. Outwardly you look like righteous people, but inwardly your hearts are filled with hypocrisy and lawlessness."What sorrow awaits you teachers of religious law and you Pharisees? Hypocrites! For you build tombs for the prophets your ancestors killed, and you decorate the monuments of the godly people your ancestors destroyed."

"But in saying that, you testify against yourselves that you are indeed the descendants of those who murdered the prophets. Go ahead and finish what your ancestors started. 33 Snakes! Sons of vipers! How will you escape the judgment of hell? As a result, you will be held responsible for the murder of all godly people of all time from the murder of righteous Abel, and murder of Zechariah son of Berekiah, whom you killed in the Temple between the sanctuary and the altar."

Jesus Grieves over Jerusalem: "O Jerusalem, Jerusalem, the city that kills the prophets and stones God's messengers! How often I have wanted to gather your children together as a hen protects her chicks beneath her wings, but you wouldn't let me.

And now, look, your house is abandoned and desolate. For I tell you this, you will never see me again until you say, 'Blessings on the one who comes in the name of the Lord!" But Jesus Christ did not come to promote religion. He did not flatter those who were religious by saying that He was glad to see their religious activities and that He, too, was a religious person. When the religious leaders complained that Jesus socialized with sinners, He replied (Luke 5:31-32), "It is not those who are well who need a physician, but those who are sick.

I have not come to call the righteous but sinners to repentance." He was not saying that some are righteous enough to get into heaven by their own good deeds. Rather, by the "righteous," He meant the self-righteous. Their pride blinded them to their sin and kept them from coming to Jesus for forgiveness and salvation. (Mark 12:17; Romans 13:1), True religion is a way of life, not just a ritual or a formality. Its members adhere to the Bible's high moral standards in all aspects of life. (Ephesians 5:3-5; 1 John 3:18). If anyone thinks he is religious and does not bridle his tongue but deceives his heart, this person's religion is worthless. Religion that is pure and undefiled before God. (Ecclesiastes 12:13) - The conclusion, when all has been heard is to fear God and keep His commandments, because this applies to every person.

WHY RELIGION (ALONE) CAN'T SAVE YOU (JOHN 3:1-7)

One of the greatest lies that Satan has foisted on humans is that religion can save you. By "Religion," I mean adherence to the beliefs and practices of a religion in the hope that your belief will gain you right standing with God. In our last study, we looked at John 2:23-25, where many believed in Jesus as they saw the signs (miracles) that He did, but Jesus didn't believe in them, because He could see the true condition of their hearts. As I explained, those verses serve as an introduction to the story of Jesus and Nicodemus.

John connects the stories by using the word "man" (or "men"). The four Gospels make it clear that the most difficult people to reach with the gospel are not the notoriously wicked.

John says (2:24) that Jesus "knew all men," and then adds (2:25), "and because He did not need anyone to testify concerning man, for He Himself knew what was in man." Remember, there were no chapter breaks in the original text, so the next verse (3:1) continues, "Now there was a man of the Pharisees, named Nicodemus." There is also a connection between the people who observed Jesus' signs (2:23) and Nicodemus' opening statement to Jesus (3:2), "no one can do these signs that you do unless God is with him." The fact that Jesus' knew all men and what was in each man is made evident in His reply to Nicodemus. Jesus could see beneath Nicodemus' religious veneer. He knew that Nicodemus' religion could not save him. He needed the new birth. This encounter teaches us that Religion can't save you because to enter God's eternal kingdom you need the new birth by the Holy Spirit. The story of Jesus' encounter with Nicodemus runs from 3:1-21, but somewhere after 3:12, Nicodemus fades out as John records Jesus' words about the Son of Man being lifted, as Moses lifted the serpent in the wilderness. The direct words of Jesus fade away after 3:15 and John's commentary runs from 3:16-21. Today we can only look at 3:1-7.

Religion can't deal with the fundamental human need to be reconciled to the holy God. This means that he belonged to the Sanhedrin, the ruling council in Jerusalem that consisted of 71 members from the Pharisees and Sadducees. The Sadducees were almost all from the aristocracy and were more political than religious. They held to some heretical religious beliefs. The Pharisees were largely middle-class businessmen who were concerned about following the Jewish law. They had separated themselves (the word Pharisee probably comes from a word meaning to separate) from the common people by their strict adherence to their many regulations and rules (Donald Hagner, The Zondervan Pictorial Encyclopedia of the Bible, by Merrill C. Tenney, 4:747). Nicodemus was apparently a leading Pharisee, because Jesus calls him "the teacher of Israel" (3:10).

John reports that Nicodemus came to Jesus by night. There have been many speculations about why he did this. Perhaps the most likely is that he was afraid of what the other members of the council would think of him. He seems to have been a rather timid man (John 7:50-52; 19:39). Some suggest that since most of John's references to "night" have a spiritual symbolism and he may be hinting at Nicodemus' spiritual condition. Although he was a religious leader, he was in spiritual darkness (D. A. Carson, The Gospel According to John (Eerdmans/Apollos), p. 186).Nicodemus seems to have been impressed by Jesus and the signs He did. For a leader of the Sanhedrin to come to the quarters of an uneducated Galilean carpenter, address Him as "Rabbi," and acknowledge that He had come from God was no small matter. Perhaps Nicodemus uses the plural "we" to refer to a few of his colleagues, but he may also be hiding behind them a bit so as not to signal too much interest on his own part (ibid., p. 187). In spite of his complimentary greetings, Nicodemus' view of Jesus fell far short of acknowledging Him as the Christ, the Son of God, which is necessary to receive eternal life (20:31).The basic error of the Pharisees was to externalize religion (William Hendriksen, (John (Baker), 1:131). They invented all sorts of man made regulations to add to the Law of Moses and took pride in their observance of them. Jesus blasted them for their hypocrisy as they fastidiously cleaned the outside of their cups and dishes, but neglected to deal with the sin in their hearts (Matt. 23:25-28). As we saw in John 2:23-25, the important thing with the Lord is what is in our hearts. He sees and judges "the thoughts and intentions of our hearts" (Heb. 4:12-13). Later, when the Pharisees questioned Jesus about why His disciples did not wash their hands according to their traditions, He blasted them (Mark 7:6-8):"Rightly did Isaiah prophesy of you hypocrites, as it is written: 'These people honour Me with their lips, but their heart is far away from Me. But in vain do they worship Me, teaching as doctrines the precepts of men.' Neglecting the commandment of God, you hold to the tradition of men." Those who are in religion deceive themselves by thinking that their outward rituals and rules will impress God, while at the same time they dodge dealing with the sin that is in their hearts. Of course, God sees right through it all. God requires "truth in the innermost being" (Ps. 51:6). So, religion cannot help just anyone gain access to heaven because religion only deals with external matters. No amount of rule-keeping or adherence to religious rituals can reconcile a sinner to the holy God. You would think that Jesus would be elated at the prospect of winning a member of the Sanhedrin as one of His followers. This guy could be a key disciple! Think of his influence! Think of how his testimony would impress the other religious leaders, not to mention the common people. Jesus showed no such excitement, no deference, and no eager politeness. There was not even any attempt at persuasiveness or accommodation. Jesus was no respecter of persons. Rather, He cut to the quick by telling Nicodemus: To be reconciled to God, you must be reborn from above. (John 3:3) "Jesus Christ answered and said to him, 'Truly, truly, I say to you, unless one is born again, he cannot see the kingdom of God.'" Jesus "answered," but Nicodemus hadn't asked a question! B. F. Westcott (Cited by Andreas Kostenberger, John (Baker), p. 121) remarked, "The Lord answered not his words, but his thoughts." Jesus knew what was in Nicodemus' heart and answered accordingly. Three times (3:3, 5, 11) in this interview Jesus uses the phrase, "Truly, truly." It transliterates the Aramaic, "Amen," which came from a verb meaning "to confirm." It was used to give assent to the words uttered by another, as we still use it today. Jesus used the phrase to give added significance and attention to what follows.

Leon Morris explains (The Gospel According to John (Eerdmans), p. 169), "It marks the words as uttered before God, who is thus invited to bring them to pass. The point that Jesus wanted to hammer home to Nicodemus is that you don't need further instruction in religion. You need to be born again! You need to see yourself as a sinner who needs more than moral or religious improvement. You need nothing less than new life from God!" As Jesus will go on to say, in effect (3:14-16), "You need to see Me as more than a religious teacher. You need to see Me as your Savior, lifted up on the cross to bring salvation to sinners." Morris puts it (p. 212), "In one sentence He sweeps away all that Nicodemus stood for, and demands that he be re-made by the power of God."

"Born again" is ambiguous and may also mean "born from above." Both are true and John may intend that we understand both meanings. William Barclay (The Gospel of John (Westminster), 1:120) captures both meanings with "reborn from above." The idea is that just as we were born physically, so we need to be born spiritually. Such a birth requires the power of God.

Nicodemus, as a Jew and a Pharisee, would have been proud of the fact that he was not a Gentile, but had been born as a Jew. Jesus shows him that being a Jew, even a religious Jew , is not enough. He needed a new birth as a spiritual child of God (John 1:12-13).Jesus says (3:3) that we must be born again to "see the kingdom of God." These verses (3:3, 5)are the only reference to the kingdom in John (except 18:36, with Pilate; 6:15, "king"). It's a major theme in the Synoptic Gospels. Here it refers to the Messianic kingdom for which all Jews hoped. Ed Blum explains (The Bible Knowledge Commentary, ed. by John F. Walvoord & Roy Zuck [Victor Books], 2:281), "The kingdom is the sphere or realm of God's authority and blessing which is now invisible but will be manifested on earth (Matt. 6:10)." To see the kingdom (3:3) is basically equal to entering the kingdom (3:5), with the slight difference that "see" implies spiritual perception (1 Cor. 2:14). Carson (p. 188) explains, "To a Jew with the background and convictions of Nicodemus, 'to see the kingdom of God' was to participate in the kingdom at the end of the age, to experience eternal, resurrection life." In order to be a proper subject in God's kingdom, you must be subject to the King, and that subjection begins here and now, not in the distant future. The problem is, those who are in the flesh are by nature hostile toward God and not able to subject themselves to God. As Paul explains (Rom. 8:6-8), "For the mind set on the flesh is death, but the mind set on the Spirit is life and peace, because the mind set on the flesh is hostile toward God; for it does not subject itself to the law of God, for it is not even able to do so, and those who are in the flesh cannot please God." John Calvin (Calvin's Commentaries (Baker), p. 108).

Thus, all the religion in the world cannot resolve our basic problem of being alienated from God, because religion is based on human work that stems from the flesh to feed our pride. To be subject to the King, we need the new birth that gives us a new nature that delights in obedience to God from the heart (Rom. 6:17-18). We need a radical transformation, not just some behavior modification. We need something that the natural man cannot produce. We need nothing less than to be reborn from above.

Nicodemus was amazed (3:7) at Jesus' radical statement that he needed to be born again. He replied (3:4), "How can a man be born when he is old? He cannot enter a second time into his mother's womb and be born, can he?" It's difficult to understand what Nicodemus meant by this question. Obviously, he did not believe that Jesus was suggesting that a person go back to the womb and be reborn physically.

John MacArthur (The Gospel According to Jesus Christ (Zondervan), p. 40) thinks that Nicodemus really meant, "I can't start all over. It's too late. I've gone too far in my current religious system to start over. There's no hope for me if I must begin from the beginning." He says that Jesus demanded that Nicodemus forsake everything he stood for, and Nicodemus knew it. Jesus says God is your father and you are his son or daughter. This is why Jesus tells the story of the Prodigal Son (Lk.15:11-32). God does not allow his children to come home if they abuse his goodness and throw a party. The concept of freedom of religion is biblical for several reasons.

First, God Himself extends a "freedom of religion" to people, and the Bible has several examples. In Matthew 19:16-23, the rich young ruler comes to Jesus. After a brief conversation, the young man "went away sorrowful," choosing not to follow Christ. The salient point here is that Jesus let him go. God does not "force" belief in Him. Faith is commanded but never coerced. In Matthew 23:37, Jesus expressed His desire to gather the children of Jerusalem to Himself, but they "were not willing." If God gives men the freedom to choose or to reject Him, then so should we.

Second, the freedom of religion respects the image of God in man (Genesis 1:26). Part of God's likeness is man's volition, i.e., the fact that man can choose.

DOES GOD OPPOSE RELIGIOUS FREEDOM IN THE OLD TESTAMENT?

A majority of modern cultures value religious freedom as one of the underpinnings of society, like the Pilgrims who founded Plymouth Colony, we see religious freedom as a basic human right. However, people sometimes wonder if religious liberty is at odds with the Old Testament Law. In Deuteronomy, God explicitly commands His people to worship Him only and to avoid any other god. In Deut. 6:14-15 He says, "Do not follow other gods, the gods of the peoples around you; for the Lord your God, who is among you, is a jealous God and his anger will burn against you, and he will destroy you from the face of the land." This seems to mean God opposes religious freedom.

There are passages in Deuteronomy that speak of destroying nations that followed other gods. Deuteronomy 7:4 also notes that the Israelites could not intermarry with people from other nations to avoid partaking of their idolatry. Christian teachings support religious freedom today. While the Bible clearly teaches there is one way to God (John 14:6) and there is a particular God to worship, no one is to be forced to believe in Jesus Christ. Instead, Jesus commanded His followers to go into all the world and make disciples by teaching and baptizing them (Matthew 28:18–20). Those who reject the message are condemned by God, but they cannot be forced to believe the teachings of Christianity or to follow them. Based on the Old Covenant, God governed His people in all matters, legal, cultural, moral, and religious. We are no longer under the Old Covenant (Galatians 5:18). Under the New Covenant, we follow the law of Christ (Galatians 6:2), but everyone is free to accept or reject Christ. There is no coercion in the gospel message, only a call to repent and believe. No human law or government has the ability to create faith in the heart, and any government that mandates faith is misguided.

The Scripture allows for people to freely choose whether to follow the teachings of Christianity with the warning that one's eternal destiny is at stake. Religion is man searching for God; Christianity is God searching for man that is why salvation is a freely given gift from God, and not based on our merits.

HOW TO BELIEVE IN GOD

Believing in God means believing in a higher power. Nearly nine-in-ten Americans (89%) say they believe in "God or a universal spirit," and most of them (63% of all adults) are absolutely certain in this belief. There has been a modest decline in the share of Americans who believe in God since the Religious Landscape Study was first conducted in 2007 (from 92% to 89%), and a bigger drop in the share of Americans who say they believe in God with absolute certainty.

Most adherents to Christian traditions say they believe in God with absolute certainty however this conviction has declined noticeably in recent years among several Christian groups. The largest drops have been among mainline Protestants (down from 73% in 2007 to 66% today), Catholics (from 72% to 64%) and Orthodox Christians (from 71% to 61%). Among non-Christians, the pattern is mixed. Most Muslims (84%) are absolutely certain that God exists, but far fewer Hindus (41%), Jews (37%) or Buddhists (29%) are certain there is a God or universal spirit.

As was the case in 2007, most religiously unaffiliated people continue to express some level of belief in God or a universal spirit. However, the share of religious "nones" who believe in God have dropped substantially in recent years (from 70% in 2007 to 61% today). Religious "nones" who believe in God are far less certain about this belief compared with those who identify with a religion. In fact, most religiously unaffiliated believers say they are less than absolutely certain about God's existence. Nearly one-in-ten U.S. adults overall (9%) now say they do not believe in God, up from 5%.

THE GLOBALISATION OF CULTURE

Cultural globalisation refers to the transmission of ideas, meanings, and values around the globe in such a way as to extend and intensify social relations. This process is binds by the common cultures that have been diffused by the Internet, popular culture media, and international travel. The Scriptures have power and, as Paul told Timothy, they "are able to make you wise for salvation through faith in Christ Jesus" (2 Tim. 3:15). Our goal must be to get people to the Scriptures. The Bible transcends culture and when people read it, they see Jesus because the Scriptures bear witness to Him (John 5:39). The Holy Spirit works through his word. Through the Scriptures, He opens the eyes of the blind so they see "the light of the knowledge of the glory of God in the face of Jesus Christ" (2 Cor. 4:6). Ugur from Turkey, Priya from India, Faisal from Pakistan, Mahmoud from Syria, Jenia from Russia, and May from China are all people who came to believe Jesus through reading the Bible. Jesus said, "Truly, truly, I say to you, whoever hears my word and believes who sent me has eternal life" (John 5:24). God saves former Muslims, Hindus, Buddhists, and more all through the power of His word. Next time you're in a Starbucks and see someone who doesn't look like you, or hear someone who doesn't sound like you, why not make a friend and over time bring him or her to the Bible? We can reach the world for Christ from our own backyards! "How beautiful are the feet of those who preach the good news" (Rom. 10:15). Globalisation results from the removal of barriers between national economies to encourage the flow of goods, services, capital, and labor. Thomas L. Friedman describes the "flattening" of the world economy through globalized trade, outsourcing, supply-chaining and political liberalisation. There has been a development of economic, political, and cultural processes to the point that they become global in scale and impact, according to the 21st Century Global Dynamics Initiative of the Mellichamp faculty cluster at the California University Santa Barbara. The global dynamics of the media have changed considerably since the turn of the twenty first century, marking what appears to be a distinctive rupture.

THE EFFECTS OF GLOBALISATION IN THE 21ST CENTURY

Globalisation of culture, the integration of world markets and mass sharing of information has left virtually no part of life in the 21st century unaffected. Fast-flowing advances in technology occurring at a lightningspeed have shifted values, eroded cultures and revolutionised the job market.In contemporary life, globalisation's innumerable effects, not all of which are positive, can be seen on every television, smart phone, and tablet.Globalisation is "the act extending an influence on all parts of the world." It involves the emergence of a single world market or deregulations resulting in internationalisation. At first glance, globalisation doesn't seem all that bad. Globalisation seems to hold an answer to the world's financial troubles, among other things. However, prayerful consideration and research reveals disturbing historical precedence. The historical form of globalisation is military conquest. The Assyrian Empire is an apt example. From the late 25th or early 24th century BC to 605 BC, the Assyrians controlled vast swaths of Babylonia, Egypt and the Holy Land. While technologically advanced for their time, the Assyrians were also brutal warriors who murdered, tortured and enslaved their enemies.

The most well-known example of historical globalisation is the attempted construction of the Tower of Babel in the 21st century BC. Rather than filling the earth as God commanded (Genesis 9:1), mankind rebelled, deciding to centralize in one city and not be scattered over the earth (Genesis 11:4). This construction effort was spearheaded by Noah's great-grandson, King Nimrod (whose name means "rebel"). God, in response, confused their languages, thus forcing the people to group together by dialect and settle (Gen.11:8-9).The empires that were presented in a dream to King Nebuchadnezzar of Babylonia represent other attempts to institute one-world government (Daniel 2). Daniel's prophetic interpretation of the king's dream is summarized our article,

'What is the meaning of Nebuchadnezzar in Daniel 2?' It is notable that Nebuchadnezzar envisioned a fifth and final world empire, which is yet to come. This final empire will be a true global government, ruled by the man known as the Antichrist, also called the beast and the lawless one (Revelation 13:4; 2 Thessalonians 2:8). He will have "authority over every tribe, people, language and nation," and he, along with the False Prophet, will force all people to take his mark. This future global leader will control all financial transactions (Revelation 13:17) and all religious observance (Revelation 13:8). Refusal to worship the Antichrist means death; acquiescence means eternal punishment from God (Revelation 13:15; 14:9-11).

The Bible, therefore, shows that any time man attempts "globalisation" it is ruled by wicked, ungodly empires. We should oppose globalisation to the extent that we understand that it is Satan, currently the god of this age (2 Corinthians 4:4). It is interesting to note that man's (and Satan's) final attempt at globalisation will include a resurgence of "Babylon," which started the globalisation effort so long ago (see Revelation 18). Also, we also know that the "whole world is a prisoner of sin" (Galatians 3:22) and that believers are to "hate evil" (Psalm 97:10).

We must shine the light of righteousness into the darkness where we find it, via the gospel message (Matthew 5:16; cf. John 8:12). It is appropriate to rebuke wickedness, and there is much of that to be found in Satan's version of globalisation. However, 1 Peter 2:13 does tell us to "submit yourselves for the Lord's sake to every authority instituted among men," and Jesus Himself warned us to "give to Caesar what is Caesar's" (Matthew 22:21), so it is required that we keep our opposition within the constraints of the law of the land.

God has a plan for globalisation under the headship of the King and Redeemer, Jesus Christ (Rev. 19–20). Evidently, there will still be individual nations under Christ's rule (Zechariah 2:10-11). The Kingdom will be a time of righteousness and true justice (Isaiah 11:3-5). How peaceful and joyful the days of Christ's Kingdom will be! and Isaiah 12:3-4 describes this for us.

THE NEW WORLD ORDER

The New World Order is a conspiracy theory which posits a new period of history bringing about a major change in the world with the balance of world power. This will be accomplished by the installation of a one-world political system. This New World Order is theorised by some to involve a group of elitist people bent on ruling the world through a single worldwide system of government. The appeal of this New World Order lies in its proposal to free the world of from war and political strife, and its promises to eradicate poverty, disease, and hunger. Its ultimate goal is a sense of unity and oneness with all people speaking the same language. Other objectives include the use of a single, world-wide currency, as well as oneness in politics, religion, and moral values. As a result, conspiracy theorists believe, the world will be under one rule, that of one government that promises worldwide peace.

The Scriptures are clear concerning all these things. As Christians, we are commanded to obey and respect those in authority, including our government. However, we can easily see that there are some severe consequences of such a New World Order, both from an economic and a religious standpoint (Romans 13:1-7; Acts 5:29).

People, who desire the ushering in of a New World Order, whether secular or religious, are in for a rude awakening. The truth is that false religious teachings cannot bring utopia into being, regardless of man's creativity and ingenuity. Only heaven brings lasting peace and happiness. The Bible makes it very clear that all things associated with this life on earth with its sufferings, its decay, its discontent, and death will continue with this physical life (2 Corinthians 4:16; Hebrews 9:27). It is also clear that all these things are completely unknown in the heavenly city (Revelation 21:3-7 and Revelation 22). They will be done away with. Yes, hope is needed but it is the hope of heaven we need, not the false hope of a New World Order.

THE DEADLIEST DISEASES IN THE WORLD

Below here is a countdown of the Top 10 Deadly Diseases in the World affecting humans everywhere. The information presented here has been compiled via the World Health Organisation (WHO)'s reported data. According to the estimates in the Causes of death 2008 update, there were 57 million deaths in the world in 2008. The broad category of all "noncommunicable diseases" killed 36 million people. Communicable diseases, maternal and perinatal conditions, and nutritional conditions killed 16 million people worldwide; and external causes of injuries killed 5 million people.

Coronary Artery Disease (CAD): CAD is a condition where vessels supplying blood to the heart become narrowed. This is commonly caused by unhealthy dieting and smoking. The World Health Organisation (WHO)estimates that CAD has claimed about 7.4 million lives in 2012. That contributes to about 12.8% of all deaths globally.

Stroke: A stroke occurs when an artery supplying blood to the brain is blocked or leaked. The oxygen-deprived cells die within minutes of the blockage. According to WHO, an estimated 6.7 million lives are lost to strokes in 2012. This contributes to about 10.8% of all deaths.

Lower Respiratory Infections (LRI): LRI includes illnesses such as influenza, bronchitis, and pneumonia. The flu season is mostly prevalent in the colder half of the year for each hemisphere. The WHO estimates that LRI contributes to about 6.1% of all deaths.

Chronic Obstructive Pulmonary Disease (COPD): This disease affects the lungs, making it more difficult for the patient to breathe. The main cause of COPD is tobacco use, including inhalation of secondhand smoke. The WHO estimates that COPD has claimed 3.28 million lives in 2012, which contributes to about 5.8% of all deaths worldwide.

Diarrheal Diseases: Diarrhea is characterized by excreting fecal matter more than three times a day. Having diarrhea over the course of a few days depletes the body of water and salt. The WHO estimates that diarrheal diseases have claimed 2.46 million lives in 2012. It is the second leading cause of death of children under 5. This contributes to about 4.3% of all deaths globally.

HIV/AIDS: AIDS is caused by the Human Immunodeficiency Virus (HIV) which is transmitted through bodily fluids. HIV enters the body and hijacks T cells which then compromise the immune system. In 2012, about 1.78 million People died due to AIDS. This contributes to about 3.1% of all deaths.

Respiratory Cancers: This class of diseases includes lung, tracheal, and bronchial cancers. The main causes of these cancers are pollution by smoking, secondhand smoking, and other carcinogens which are waste by-products. 1.39 million died in 2012 from respiratory cancers which contributes to about 2.4% of all deaths.

Tuberculosis: Tuberculosis (TB) is a bacterial infection caused by Mycobacterium tuberculosis. Contraction of TB is airborne, but it is difficult to get. It is one of the leading causes of death for people with HIV. An estimated 1.34 million people have fallen to TB in 2012, contributing to about 2.4% of all deaths.

Diabetes Mellitus: Diabetes Mellitus Type I is characterized by the pancreatic cells no longer producing insulin or the production is miniscule. In type II diabetes, cells lose sensitivity to insulin, thereby becoming resilient. Type I diabetes cannot be cured, but type II diabetes can be maintained with a proper diet and exercise. An estimated 1.26 million people have lost their lives to complications with diabetes in 2012, which contributes to about 2.2% of all deaths.

Preterm Birth Complications: Although not a disease, an estimated 1 million infants are lost to due to pre-maturity and low birth weight. Most deaths occur after the first week of conceiving. These complications mostly affect developing countries where medical care is not available or is difficult to reach.

WHAT DOES THE BIBLE SAY ABOUT PANDEMIC DISEASES/SICKNESSES?

In the recent past, the ebola outbreak has prompted many to ask why God allows pandemic diseases to occur, and whether such pandemic diseases are a sign of the end times. The Bible, particularly the Old Testament, describes numerous occasions when God brought plagues and diseases on both His people and His enemies "to make you see my power" (Exodus 9:14, 16). He used plagues in Egypt to force the Pharaoh to free the Israelites from bondage, while sparing His people from being affected by them (Exodus 12:13; 15:26). This indicates His sovereign control over diseases and other afflictions.

God also warned His people of the consequences of disobedience, including plagues (Lev. 26:21-25). Numbers 16:49 and 25:9 describe God destroying 14,700 people and 24,000 people, respectively, for various acts of disobedience. After giving the Mosaic Law, God commanded the people to obey or suffer many evils, including something that sounds very similar to Ebola: "The Lord will strike you with wasting disease, with fever and inflammation plague you until you perish" (Deut.28:22). These are just a few examples of many plagues and diseases God caused.

It's sometimes hard to reconcile our loving and merciful God with displays of such wrath and anger toward His people. However God's punishments always have the goal of repentance and restoration. In 2 Chronicles 7:13-14, God said to Solomon: "When I shut up the heavens so that there is no rain, or command locusts to devour the land or send a plague among my people, if my people, who are called by my name, will humble themselves and pray and seek my face and turn from their wicked ways, then will I hear from heaven and will forgive their sin and will heal their land." Here we see God using disaster to draw us to Himself.

In the New Testament, Jesus healed "every disease and every sickness," as well as plagues in the areas He visited (Matthew 9:35; 10:1; Mark 3:10). Just as God chose to use plagues/ disease to show His power to the Israelites, Jesus healed as an exhibition of the same power to verify that He was truly the Son of God. He gave the same healing power to the disciples to verify their ministry (Luke 9:1). God still allows sickness for His own purposes, but sometimes disease, even worldwide pandemics, are simply the result of living in a fallen world. There is no way to determine which, although we do know that God has sovereign control over all things (Romans 11:36. He will work all things together for the good of those who know and love Him (Romans 8:28). The current Ebola epidemic is not the last we will see of plagues/pandemic diseases. Jesus referred to future plagues that will be part of the end-times scenario (LK. 21:11). The two witnesses of Revelation 11 will have power "to strike the earth with plague as often as they want" (Revelation 11:6). Revelation 15 speaks of seven plagues wielded by seven angels as the final, most severe judgments, described in Revelation 16. Whether the current outbreak of Ebola and other pandemic diseases are part of God's judgment, the result of living in a fallen, sinful world, or a signal that the end time is beginning, our response should be the same. For those who do not know Jesus Christ as Savior, disease is a message that helps people remember that life on this earth is tenuous and can be lost at any moment. Without the saving blood of Christ shed for us, we will pay for our sins for all eternity in a hell that will make the worst pandemic seem mild. For the Christian, however, we have the assurance of salvation and the hope of eternity because of what Christ suffered on the cross for us (Isaiah 53:5; 2 Corinthians 5:21).

WHAT DOES THE BIBLE SAY ABOUT COPING/ DEALING WITH A TERMINAL ILLNESS?

It is very difficult to accept some of the sorrowful that brings life to an end. There are few things that can stir the human soul more than the news of a terminal illness diagnosis. First of all, know that Jesus cares. Our Savior wept when His beloved friend Lazarus died and (Jn. 11:35) His heart was touched by the sorrow of Jairus' family (Luke 8:41-42).

Jesus not only cares: He is at hand to help His children. Our God is an "ever-present help in trouble" (Psalm 46:1). The Holy Spirit, dwells with us, and He will never leave (John 14:16).Jesus told us in this world we would have trouble (John 16:33), and absolutely no one is spared (Romans 5:12). Yet coping with any degree of suffering becomes easier when we understand God's overall design to redeem our fallen world.

We may not be guaranteed physical health in this life, but those who trust in God are promised spiritual security for all eternity (John10:27). Nothing can touch the soul. It is good to remember that not everything bad that happens to us is a direct result of our sin. Having a terminal illness is not proof of God's judgment on an individual. Remember the time Jesus/ His disciples came upon a man who had been blind since birth? They asked Jesus, "Rabbi, who sinned, this man or his parents, that he was born blind?"

Jesus responded, "Neither this man nor his parents sinned. This happened so that the work of God might be displayed in his life" (John 9:2-3, emphasis added). Likewise, Job's three friends were certain that his calamity resulted from sin in his life. Like Christ's disciples, they were very wrong. We may never understand the reasons for our particular trials this side of eternity, but one thing is clear: for those who love God, trials work for them, not against them (Romans 8:28).

Our earthly life is a "mist" at best, and that's why God has set eternity in our hearts (Eccl.3:11). How we react to our trials, including the trial of terminal illness reveals exactly what our faith is like. Scripture teaches us to offer our bodies as living sacrifices (Romans 12:1). In fact, "dying to self" is a requirement for those who seek to follow Jesus Christ (Luke 14:27). This means we completely subordinate our desires to those of our Lord. Like Christ at Gethsemane, "my" will needs to become "Thy" will. The author of Hebrews exhorts us to consider the suffering our Savior endured so that we ourselves do not grow weary and lose heart in our own trials. It was "For the joy set before Him" that Christ was able to endure the suffering of the cross. This "joy," for Christ, was in obeying His Father's will (Psalm 40:8), reconciling His Father with His creation, and being exalted to the right hand of the throne of God. Likewise, our own trials can be made more bearable when we consider the "joy" set before us. Our joy may come in understanding that it is through testing that God transforms us into the likeness of His Son (Job 23:10; Romans 8:29). What we see as pain, discomfort and uncertainty is our sovereign Father, who ordains or allows every event during our time on earth, to see us through a transformation. Our suffering is never meaningless. God uses suffering to change us, to minister to others, and, ultimately, to bring glory to His name. Paul reminds Christ's followers' that our earthly troubles, which last only a short time, pale in comparison to our eternal glory (2 Corinthians 4:17-18). Commenting on these verses, one theologian stated, "God will never be a debtor to anyone. We endure for His sake and by His Spirit, He will amply reward out of all proportion to what we suffered."

HOW CAN A CHRISTIAN COPE WHILE SUFFERING WITH A DEGENERATIVE DISEASE?

The Scripture tells us that "we are God's handiwork, created in to do good work, which God has prepared in advance for us to do" (Ephesians

2:10). A disease does not change this truth. God still has a purpose for those suffering with degenerative diseases. This disease is not a surprise to Him. He has known all along and has made provision for you. Staying grounded in God's Word, particularly His promises, is very helpful in coping. Keep praying. Call out to God and "cast all your anxiety on him because he cares for you" (1 Peter 5:7). It is okay to be real with God about your emotions, while also remembering the truth of who He is. The Psalms are an excellent example of this type of prayer. It is also important to stay connected with the Christian community. Romans 12:15 tells us to "rejoice with those who rejoice; mourn with those who mourn." It is important to share your burden with the body of Christ so they can provide help. A degenerative disease can feel consuming. It is easy to begin to identify as the disease rather than as a person. This is part of the reason it is important to maintain social connections, especially with fellow believers. Christian fellowship is important for the whole body of Christ (Hebrews 10:24–25). Having a disease does not make a person any less needed in the functioning of the body.

Keep engaging in hobbies, continue to meet with friends, continue to serve. Faith tells us that God has a plan during the world's fallenness, and ultimately God will create the world anew, seek to live life to the fullest in Christ (John.10:10).

"God has called me heavenward in Christ Jesus" (Philippians 3:14) and is it sometimes God's will for believers to be sick? The biblical doctrine of the sovereignty of God states that God is almighty. He is in complete control of all things, past, present and future. Nothing happens that is out of His jurisdiction. Either He directly causes, or passively allows everything that happens. Allowing something to happen and causing something to happen are two different things. Sickness is one manifestation of the two broad types of evil moral and natural. Moral evil is man's inhumanity to man. Natural evil is composed of things like natural disasters and physical sickness. Evil itself is a perversion or corruption of something that was originally good, but is now missing something. In the case of sickness, illness is a state where good health is missing. Romans 8:20-22 says, "For the creation was subjected to frustration, not by its own choice, but by the will of the one who subjected it, in hope that the creation itself will be liberated from its bondage to decay and brought into the glorious freedom of the children of God. We know that the whole of creation has been groaning in the pains of childbirth right up to the present time." Jesus went through Israel healing all manner of sickness and disease (Matthew 4:23) and even raised Lazarus from the dead after illness killed him. At other times, God uses sickness as a method of discipline or as a judgment against sin. King Uzziah in the Old Testament was struck with leprosy (2 Chronicles 26:19-20).

Nebuchadnezzar was driven to madness by God until he came to understand "the Most High rules in the affairs of men" (Daniel 4). Herod was struck down and worms eat him because he took God's glory upon himself (Acts 12:21-23). There is even at least one case where God allowed disease blindness not as punishment for sin, but to reveal Himself and His mighty works through that blindness (John 9:1-3).

WHY DOES GOD ALLOW SICKNESS?

The issue of sickness is always a difficult one to deal with. The key is remembering that God's ways are higher than our ways (Isaiah 55:9) when we are suffering with a sickness, disease, or injury. Romans 8:28 reminds us that God can bring about good from any situation. Many people look back on times of sickness as times when they grew closer to God, learned to trust Him more, and learned how to truly value life. This is the perspective God has because He is sovereign and knows the end result.

This does not mean sickness is always from God or that God always inflicts us with sickness to teach us a spiritual lesson. In a world tainted by sin, sickness, disease, and death will always be with us. We are fallen beings, with physical bodies prone to disease and illness. Some sickness is simply a result of the natural course of things in this world. Sickness can also be the result of a demonic attack. The Bible describes several instances when physical suffering was caused by Satan and his demons (Matt. 17:14-18; Luke 13:10-16). Some sickness is not from God, but from Satan. Even in these instances, God is still in control. God sometimes allows sin and/or Satan to cause physical suffering. Even when sickness is not directly from God, He will still use it according to His perfect will.

It is undeniable, that God sometimes intentionally allows, or even causes sickness to accomplish His sovereign purposes. While sickness is not directly addressed in the passage, Hebrews 12:5-11 describes God disciplining us to "produce a harvest of righteousness" (verse 11). Sickness can be a means of God's loving discipline. It is difficult for us to comprehend why God would work in this manner. The clearest example of this in Scripture is found is Psalm 119, in the progression through verses 67, 71, and 75. The author of Psalm 119 was looking at suffering from God's perspective.

Moral evil is the immorality and pain and suffering and tragedy that come because we choose to be selfish, arrogant, uncaring, hateful and abusive. Romans 3:23 says "All have sinned and fall short of the glory of God." The Bible says it's because of sin that nature was corrupted and "thorns and thistles" entered the world. Rom. 8:22 says, "We know that the whole creation has been groaning as in the pains of childbirth right up to the present time." In other words, nature longs for redemption to come and for things to be set right. That's the source of disorder and chaos. Paul also wrote in Romans 8: 18 that "I consider that our present sufferings are not worth comparing with the glory that will be revealed in us." Let the words of First Corinthians 2:9 soak into your soul: "No eye has seen; no ear has heard."

GOD KNEW US BEFORE WE WERE BORN

God knew what He was doing from the very beginning. He decided from the outset to shape the lives of those who love him along the same lines as the life of His Son. The Son stands first in the line of humanity He restored. We see the original and intended shape of our lives there in Him. He knows us far better than we know ourselves, our conditions, if we are pregnant, and whether we are present. That's why we can be so sure that every detail in our lives of love for God is worked into something good. God knew what He was doing from the very beginning. He decided from the outset to shape the lives of those who love him along the same lines as the life of his Son. The Son stands first in the line of humanity he restored. We see the original and intended shape of our lives there in Him.

After God made that decision of what His children should be like, He followed it up by calling people by name. After He called them by name, He set them with a solid relationship to Himself. Then, after getting them established, He stayed with them to the end, gloriously completing what He had begun. So, what do you think? With God on our side like this, how can we lose? If God didn't hesitate to put everything on the line for us, embracing our conditions and exposing Himself to the worst by sending His own Son, is there anything else He wouldn't gladly and freely do for us?

Who would dare tangle with God by messing with one of God's chosen? Who would dare even to point a finger? The one who died for us, who was raised to life for us, who is in the presence of God at this very moment sticking up for us. They kill us in cold blood because they hate you. We're sitting ducks: they pick us off one by one. Yet none of this fazes us because Jesus loves us. The word of the Lord came to Jeremiah, saying, "Before I formed you in the womb I knew you, and before you were born I consecrated you; I appointed you a prophet to the nations." Then he said, "Ah, Lord God! Behold, I do not know how to speak, for I am only a youth." But the Lord said to him, "Do not say, 'I am only a youth '" (Jer.1: 1-7). God knew His children in advance, and he chose them to become like His Son.

THE PEOPLE WHO KNOW THEIR GOD

Scripture declares that "the people who know their God will display strength and take action" (Daniel 11:32). That is a great promise. In order to understand it we need to know a little Jewish history. The Jewish people have experienced some fierce persecutions through the centuries, but none worse than under Antiochus Epiphanes, the Syrian king who reigned from 175 to 164 B.C. He assumed the name Theos Epiphanes which means "the manifest God," but the Jews changed one letter in his name (in their language) and called him Epimanes, which means "mad man." And mad he was! His hatred for the Jews was literally insane.

Daniel himself was a man who knew God. When the presidents and princes of the Medo Persian Empire prevailed upon King Darius to issue a decree prohibiting anybody from making petitions to any god or man except the king, or be cast into the lion's den, Daniel went right on praying to the God of Heaven (Daniel 6:4-15). Not even the threat of death could keep him from it. He knew his God, and people who know God have the courage and strength to do His will even though the whole world may be against them and everybody around them may be giving in to sin. We too can have the spiritual power to do God's will and to make a significant impact on the godless world in which we live. As our knowledge of Him increases and our friendship with Him grows more intimate, He makes His power more readily available to us.

Daniel anticipated this reign prophetically in this eleventh chapter of the book, and King Darius did exactly what Daniel predicted. He ordered the Jewish sacrifices to cease and polluted the temple of God by offering swine's flesh on the altar. In addition to that, he prohibited the observance of the Sabbath and the circumcision of children, ordered all copies of Scripture destroyed, set up idolatrous altars, commanded the Jews to offer unclean sacrifices and insisted that they eat swine's flesh. Anyone who disobeyed these edicts were sentenced to death. It was an ancient holocaust. As Daniel anticipated this atrocity he asked himself how these people would ever be able to survive. The answer was not long in coming: "the people who know their God will display strength and take action" (11:32). Peter tells us about people who know God. He says, "Grace and peace be multiplied to you in the knowledge of God and of Jesus our Lord" (2 Peter 1:2). His statement reveals that both grace and peace are increased in the believer's life by the full or thorough knowledge of God. Grace is God's favor, His gracious care, faithful assistance, and help. We enjoy God's help to the extent that we know Him. That should be easy to understand. If we do not know Him very well, we will not know what help He has available, or even that He is offering us any help. We must know Him in order to be able to accept the benefits He extends to us.

There is a great illustration in the book of Daniel of the peace that comes from knowing God. King Nebuchadnezzar had erected a ninety-foot statue of himself before which all his subjects were commanded to bow. To refuse meant death in the fiery furnace. Shadrach, Meshach, and Abednego were men who knew God. They could not bow before that golden image. When it became obvious that they had refused, they were brought before the king and given one last chance to do so. Nebuchadnezzar proudly announced, "if you will not worship, you will immediately be cast into the midst of a furnace of blazing fire; who can deliver you out of my hands?" (Dan.3:15).

Paul was a man who enjoyed the benefits of knowing God, and he longed for his converts to share those same blessings. He often prayed to that end, and in those prayers, we learn more about the advantages of knowing God. For the Ephesians he prayed, "That the God of our

Lord Jesus Christ, the Father of glory, may give you a spirit of wisdom and the knowledge of Him" (Ephesians 1:17). The word spirit in this instance is not a reference to the Holy Spirit.

Paul was referring to a mental attitude of true spiritual understanding which the Holy Spirit alone could produce in them, that is, the ability to comprehend God's truth and appropriate it. John and Peter were men that had this ability. They preached about Christ in the temple courtyard and the Jewish religious leaders were furious. They took the two disciples into custody and questioned them about their activities, insisting that they reveal by what power they performed their miracles. Then Peter, filled with the Holy Spirit, delivered a powerful testimony to the person of Christ, that demonstrated not only his familiarity with recent events in Jerusalem, but also his grasp of Old Testament Scripture (Acts 4:8-12). It was an amazingly articulate expression of faith from an uneducated fisherman. Where did he get that kind of wisdom? The record goes on to tell us: the Jews "began to recognize them as having been with Jesus" (Acts 4:13). They had come into a personal and intimate knowledge of the living God through His Son Jesus Christ. They had walked with Him and talked with Him for three and one-half years. As a result they had an understanding of spiritual truth that those religious rulers could not begin to match with all their theological training and sanctimonious religiosity. People who know God have wisdom.

A Psalm writer named Asaph did although he was initially in a bad shape spiritually. He says he came close to stumbling; his steps had almost slipped (Psalm 73:2). He was on the verge of a serious spiritual defeat, angry with God because ungodly people were doing better than he was. Being in the sanctuary of God was an Old Testament way of expressing fellowship with Him. Asaph got to know God with His love, His care, His guidance, and His all-sufficiency. Paul wrote to them, "But now that you have come to know God, or rather to be known by God, how is it that you turn back again to the weak and worthless elemental things, to which you desire to be enslaved all over again?" (Galatians 4:9). They came to know God and their knowledge had delivered them from bondage. As sad as it was, they had willfully chosen to put themselves back under the very bondage from which they had been delivered. Why? What was their problem? The book of Daniel tells us of what appear to be two instances of a fourth man who, "like a son of the God" (3:25), walked with Daniel's three friends in the furnace? Who was the angel whom God sent to shut the lions' mouths when Daniel was in their den (6:22)? The Lord Jesus Christ is now absent from us in body, but spiritually it makes no difference. Still, we may find and know God through seeking and finding His company.

HOW DID PEOPLE KNOW ABOUT GOD BEFORE THE BIBLE?

The Old Testament was completed around 400 BC. The New Testament was completed by AD 100. How did people know about God before this time? Romans 1:19 offers one way people had evidence about a Creator God prior to the Bible: "For what can be known about God is plain to them, because God has shown it to them." One example of this is the human conscience, which includes a universal sense of right and wrong among all people. Not every person agrees on what is right and wrong, but every person is designed with a sense of morality. This sense of morality points toward God.

Romans 1:20 offers another insight into how people would have understood God prior to the writing of the Bible's books. It notes, "For his invisible attributes, namely, his eternal power and divine nature, have been clearly perceived, ever since the creation of the world, in the things that have been made. So, they are without excuse." The creation around us offers ample evidence of a Creator (Ps. 19:1-4). The complexity of the universe also points toward a designer. From the exquisite design of a flower to the human body, each detail points toward an ultimate

Designer who designed with purpose, care, and wisdom. In addition to these areas of general revelation available to all people, God has communicated revelation about Himself through other means than the Bible at times. For example, the Bible speaks of times when people cast lots to determine God's will (Acts 1:21-26; Proverbs 16:33). Urim and Thummin were special types of this lot used by the High Priest (Exodus 28:30).

God also used visions and dreams as ways to communicate to people. These were especially prevalent in Genesis (Genesis 20:3-7; 31:11-13). Prophets often communicated through spoken words to people, including Jonah who spoke to a non-Jewish people to save an entire city. Angels are also often recorded in the Bible as ministering spirits who communicated God's messages to individuals. While God has spoken clearly and directly through Scripture, He has often communicated through both natural and supernatural means as He has seen fit to share revelation with others.

In addition, the Bible shares the message of God communicating directly through Jesus coming to earth to live among us (John 1:1-14) and offering eternal life to all who believe (John 3:16).

HOW CAN I COME TO REALLY KNOW GOD?

Actually knowing God begins with accepting His salvation. Without the sacrifice of Jesus, we are dead in sin (Colossians 2:13). A dead person cannot raise himself to life in order to come to know anyone. However, once we have accepted the gift of Christ through faith, we can begin to truly know God. The wonder of salvation is that we are not only saved out of an eternity in hell, but to a life in Christ. We are invited into fellowship with God (John 17:20-26) and made part of His family (Romans 8:15-17). After salvation, knowing God starts with hearing what He has to say about Himself. Though we cannot know God fully in this lifetime (Isaiah 55:8-9; 1 Corinthians 13:12), we can know Him in part. He has revealed certain things about Himself to us.

We find these revelations in God's written Word (the Bible) and the Word incarnate (Jesus). We also glean them through creation, which is His general revelation to all (Rom.1:20). Believers have been given the Holy Spirit so that we can make sense of God's Word and perceive the things He reveals to us (John 16:13).God desires to have a personal and intimate relationship with us. We ask God for His guidance, "ask, and it will be given to you; seek, and you will find; knock, and it will be opened to you. For everyone who asks receives, and the one who seeks finds, and to the one who knocks it will be opened" (Luke 11:9-10). We have been invited to seek God. We can do so boldly (Hebrews 4:16). We also come to know God by obeying Him. Jesus said, "Abide in me, and I in you. As the branch cannot bear fruit by itself, unless it abides in the vine, neither can you, unless you abide in me. You are my friends if you do what I command you. You did not choose me, but I chose you and appointed you that you should go and bear fruit and that your fruit should abide, so that whatever you ask the Father in my name, he may give it to you. These things I command you, so that you will love one another" (John 15:4, 14, 16-17).

When we obey someone, we begin to understand his desires. When we obey God, we also experience the blessings He has for us because His commands are meant for our good. Abiding in God is one way we come to know Him (Matthew 12:33; Galatians 5:22-24; Ephesians 2:10). All people desire to know their Creator, even if they are not professed believers in God. Today we are bombarded with advertising that promises many ways to satisfy our cravings to know more, have more and be more. However, the empty promises that come from the world will never satisfy in the way that knowing God will satisfy. Jesus said, "Now this is eternal life: that they may know you, the only true God, and Jesus Christ, whom you have sent" (John 17:3). The key to truly knowing God is very imperative to understand that man, on his own, is incapable of truly knowing God because of man's sinfulness. God unless we accept and receive the promise of Jesus' sacrifice on the cross.

So, in order to truly know God, we must first receive Him into our lives. "As many as received Him, to them He gave the right to become children of God, even to those who believe in His name" (John 1:12). Nothing is of greater importance than understanding this truth when it comes to knowing God. Jesus makes it clear that He alone is the way to heaven and to a personal knowledge of God: "I am the way, and the truth, and the life; no one comes to the Father, but through Me" (John 14:6).Paul writes to Timothy, "As for you, continue in what you have learned and have become convinced of, because you know those from whom you learned it, and how from infancy you have known the Holy Scriptures, which are able to make you wise for salvation through faith in Christ Jesus. All Scripture is God-breathed and is useful for teaching, rebuking, correcting and training in righteousness, so that the man of God may be thoroughly equipped for every good work" (2 Timothy 3:14-16).

After all, we were created to do good work (Eph.2:10), in order to be part of God's plan of continuing to reveal Himself to the world. We carry the responsibility to live out the very faith that is required to know God. We are salt and light on this earth (Matthew 5:13-14), designed to bring God's flavor to the world and to serve as a shining light in the midst of darkness.

THE UNKNOWN GOD IN ACTS 17:23

In Acts 17, Paul arrives in Athens, the citadel of the many Greek gods. In the city was the Areopagus, or Mars Hill, where a council of civic leaders met. This council had charge of religious and educational matters in Athens. While in Athens, Paul was provoked by the many idols he saw. The Epicureans were followers of Epicurus (341—270 BC), who taught that happiness, was the ultimate goal in life. The Stoic thinkers regarded Zeno (340—265 BC) as their founder. He was noted for promoting the rational over the emotional. Hearing Paul teach about Jesus, the philosophers had Paul come to the Areopagus and asked him to tell them about this "new," strange teaching he was proclaiming. Standing in the midst of the Areopagus, Paul could tell that the Athenians who had gathered were very religious, having seen their many objects of worship. One altar among the many caught his attention. On it were inscribed the words "TO AN UNKNOWN GOD." In their ignorance, the Greeks had erected an altar to whatever god they might have inadvertently left out of their pantheon. Paul masterfully uses this altar as an opportunity to share the one true God.

In the intervening period, the Greeks obviously didn't know who this god was. Paul explained to them that this "unknown god" was the biblical God, the Creator of heaven and earth, who does not dwell in temples made with hands. God is the Source of life for all nations, and He is really the One they were funwittingly seeking. Paul says God is near; in fact, "in him we live and move and have our being" (Acts 17:27–28). The Greeks, however, were unable to find the true God on their own, so God came searching for them. He calls all men to repent and accept Jesus Christ, who was raised from the dead and will judge the world in righteousness (Luke 10:22) (Acts 17:19, 22). Ares was the Greek god of war, and according to Greek mythology this hill was the place where Ares stood trial before the other gods for the murder of Poseidon's son Alirrothios. Rising some 377 feet above the land below and not far from the Acropolis and Agora (marketplace), Mars Hill served as the meeting place for the Areopagus Court, the highest court in Greece for civil, criminal, and religious matters. The biblical significance of Mars Hill is that it is the location of one of Paul's most important gospel presentations at the time of his visit to Athens during his second missionary journey (Acts 17:16–34). It was where he addressed the religious idolatry of the Greeks who even had an altar to the "Unknown God." It was this altar and their religious idolatry that Paul used as a starting point in proclaiming to them the one true God and how they could be reconciled to Him. Paul's sermon is a classic example of a gospel presentation that presents the gospel message in a logical and biblical fashion. In many ways it is a classic example of apologetics in action. Paul started his message by addressing the false beliefs of those gathered there that day and then used those beliefs as a way of presenting the gospel message to them. We know that when Paul arrived in Athens he found "a city full of idols" (Acts 17: 16). In his usual manner, Paul began presenting the gospel to both Jews and Gentiles. He started by "reasoning in the synagogue with the Jews and with the Gentile worshipers" (Acts 17: 17). He then also proclaimed the gospel "in the marketplace daily with those who happened to be there" (Acts 17:17). While in the marketplace he encountered some Epicurean and Stoic philosophers (Acts 17:18) who, having heard Paul proclaim the resurrected Jesus Christ, wanted to learn about "this new doctrine" he was teaching, so they "brought him to the Areopagus" to hear more from him (Acts 17:19–20).

We know from history that the Epicurean philosophers generally believed that God existed but that He was not interested or involved with humanity. On the other hand, the Stoic philosophers had the worldview that "God was the world's soul" and that the goal of life was "to rise above all things" so that one showed no emotional response to either pain or pleasure. These groups, with opposing world views, loved to debate philosophy and religion. They considered Paul's "babblings" about the resurrection of Christ, they brought him to the Areopagus and "spent their time in discussion ."

As stated earlier, Paul's presentation of the gospel is a great example for us, both as a pattern for how Paul identified with his audience and as an example of apologetics in action. His connection with his audience is seen in how he begins addressing those gathered at the Areopagus. He begins with the observation that they were "very religious," based on the fact that they had many altars and "objects of worship" (Acts 17:23) including an altar to "the Unknown God." Paul uses that altar to introduce them to the one true God and the only way of salvation,

Jesus Christ. His apologetic method and his knowledge that they did not even know what God is really like leads him to go back to Genesis and to the beginning of creation. Having a completely wrong view of God, those gathered that day needed to hear what God really was like before they would understand the message of the gospel. Paul begins explaining to them the sovereign God who created all things and gives life and breath to all things. He continues to explain that it was God who created from one individual all men and nations and even appointed the time and boundaries of their dwelling (Acts 17:26). His message continues as he explains the closeness of God and their need to repent of their rebellion against Him. Paul completes his message by introducing them to the One before whom they would all stand one day and be judged—Jesus Christ, whom God had raised from the dead. Many in the audience scoffed at the idea that Christ was crucified and rose from the dead on the third day because the idea of the resurrection to the Greeks was foolishness (1 Corinthians 1:23). Yet a few believed what Paul said and joined him.

What happened on Mars Hill is important because of the many lessons that can be learned, not only from how Paul presented the gospel and a biblical worldview, but also in the varied responses he received.

As with all men, those who were confronted with the truth of the gospel and did not respond in faith had no guarantee of a second chance. As Hebrews 3:15 says, "Today if you will hear His voice, do not harden your hearts as in rebellion."

LIVING IN A WORLD OF LIES

Paul's message to the philosophers that day ended with a call to repentance and acceptance of the two fundamental truths. Worldliness is simply putting your attention on yourself and the desires of the flesh that you crave. Sexual temptation is rampant, and it is easy for someone who is weak to want those desires fulfilled. If putting another "notch on your belt" makes you feel like a man, you are living for the world.

1 John 2:16-17 says, "For all that is in the world – the desires of the flesh and the desires of the eyes and the pride of life – is not from the Father but is from the world. And the world is passing away along with its desires, but whoever does the will of God abides forever." Romans 12:2 says, "Do not be conformed to this world, but be transformed by the renewal of your mind, that by testing you may discern what is the will of God, what is good and acceptable and perfect."

Jesus calls us to be unselfish and to help others. In fact, "He said to him (a Pharisee lawyer) you shall love the Lord your God with all your heart and with all your soul and with all your mind. This is the great and first commandment. And a second is like it: You shall love your neighbor as yourself." (Matt.22:37-39) You see, you must die to your own desires in order to stop being of the world. You must show love to those around you and help them, instead of helping yourself. The more you put to death your own desires of the flesh, the more you will also start living to help others and show them love.

Do not lay up for yourselves treasures on earth, where moth and rust destroy and where thieves break in and steal, but lay up for yourselves treasures in Heaven, where neither Moth nor rust destroys and where thieves do not break in and steal.

When Scripture talks about darkness usually it is referring to a sinful path. Jesus is the light and Satan is darkness. Spiritually blind people are living in darkness. They can't understand the gospel or biblical things. They are blind and they can't see that they're on the path that leads to hell. Isaiah 45:7-8 states "I create the light and make the darkness. I send good times and bad times. I, the LORD, am the one who does these things. Open up, O heavens, and pour out your righteousness. Let the earth open wide so salvation and righteousness can sprout up together. I, the LORD, created them." (Psalm 104:19-20) You made the moon to mark the seasons, and the sun knows when to set. You send the darkness, and it becomes night, when all the forest animals prowl about. (John 1:4-5) The Word gave life to everything that was created, and his life brought light to everyone. The light shines in the darkness, and the darkness can never extinguish it. (John 3:19-20) and the judgment are based on this fact: God's light came into the world, but people loved the darkness more than the light, for their actions were evil. All who do evil hate the light and refuse to go near it for fear their sins will be exposed. (1 John 1:5) This is the message we heard from Jesus and now declare to you.

Matthew 6:22-23 "The eye is the lamp of the body. If your eyes are healthy, your whole body will be full of light. But if your eyes are unhealthy, your whole body will be full of darkness. If then the light within you is darkness, how great is that darkness!" (Isaiah 5:20). How horrible it will be for those who call evil good and good evil, who turn darkness into light and light into darkness, who turn what is bitter into something sweet and what is sweet into something bitter. Proverbs 2:13-14 these men turn from the right way to walk down dark paths. They take pleasure in doing wrong, and they enjoy the twisted ways of evil.

Psalm 82:5 But these oppressors know nothing; they are so ignorant! They wander about in darkness, while the whole world is shaken to the core. 1 John 1:6 If we claim that we have fellowship with him but keep living in darkness, we are lying and not practicing the truth. John 12:35 Then Jesus told them, "You are going to have the light just a little while longer. Walk while you have the light, before darkness overtakes you. Whoever walks in the dark does not know where they are going. 1 John 2:4 whoever says, "I know him," but does not do what he commands is a liar, and the truth is not in that person. Proverbs 4:19 But the way of the wicked is like total darkness. They have no idea what they are stumbling over.

John 11:10 But at night there is danger of stumbling because they have no light."2 Corinthians 4:4 in whom the god of this world hath blinded the minds of them which believe not, lest the light of the glorious gospel of Christ, who is the image of God, should shine unto them. 1 John 2:11 But anyone who hates another brother or sister is still living and walking in darkness. Such a person does not know the way to go, having been blinded by the darkness.

Ephesians 5:11 Have nothing to do with the fruitless deeds of darkness, but rather expose them.

Romans 13:12 the night is almost gone; the day of salvation will soon be here. So remove your dark deeds like dirty clothes, and put on the shining armor of right living.

(2 Corinthians 6:14) Don't team up with those who are unbelievers. How can righteousness be a partner with wickedness? How can light live with darkness? Eccl. 2:13-14 I thought, "Wisdom is better than foolishness, just as light is better than darkness. For the wise can see where they are going, but fools walk in the dark."

Salvation brings light to people who are in the dark. Repent and trust in Christ alone (Isa.9:2). The people walking in darkness have seen a great light; a light has dawned on those living in the land of darkness. You have enlarged the nation and increased its joy. The people have rejoiced before You as they rejoice at harvest time and as they rejoice when dividing spoils.23. Acts 26:16-18 now get to your feet! For I have appeared to you to appoint you as my servant and witness. You are to tell the world what you have seen and what I will show you in the future. And I will rescue you from both your own people and the Gentiles. Yes, I am sending you to the Gentiles to open their eyes, so they may turn from darkness to light and from the power of Satan to God. Then they will receive forgiveness for their sins and be given a place among God's people, who are set apart by faith in me.' Colossians 1:12-15 always thanking the Father. He has enabled you to share in the inheritance that belongs to his people, who live in the light. For he has rescued us from the kingdom of darkness and transferred us into the Kingdom of his dear Son, who purchased our freedom and forgave our sins. Christ is the visible image of the invisible God. He existed before anything was created and is supreme over all creation, John 8:12 When Jesus spoke again to the people, he said, "I am the light of the world. Whoever follows me will never walk in darkness, but will have the light of life." Ephesians 5:8-9 For once you were full of darkness, but now you have light from the Lord. So live as people of light! For this light within you produces only what is good and right and true. Jude 1:13 They are like wild waves of the sea, churning up the foam of their shameful deeds. They are like wandering stars, doomed forever to blackest darkness. Matthew 8:12 But many Israelites–those for whom the Kingdom was prepared–will be thrown into outer darkness, where there will be weeping and gnashing of teeth." (2 Peter 2:4-6) He threw them into hell, in gloomy pits of darkness, where they are being held until the day of judgment. God did not spare the ancient world except for Noah and the seven others in his family. Noah warned the world of God's righteous judgment. God protected Noah when he destroyed the world of ungodly people with a vast flood. Later, God condemned the cities of Sodom and Gomorrah and turned them into heaps of ashes. He made them an example of what will happen to ungodly people. Eph. 6:12 outlines how "we wrestle not against flesh and blood, but against principalities, against powers, against the rulers of the darkness of this world, against spiritual wickedness in high places."

THE NINTH COMMANDMENT

Enshrined in the Ten Commandments is a decree from God against lying. The ninth point states, "You shall not bear false witness against your neighbor" (Exodus 20:16; Deuteronomy 5:20). Certainly, this means we are not to commit perjury by giving false testimony before a judicial body about others. This law protects every upright and decent person's reputation against slander despicable lies invented and disseminated to harm others. Exodus 23:1 says, "You shall not circulate a false report. Do not put your hand with the wicked to be an unrighteous witness". A thief steals only material items. But a slanderer may rob a man of his reputation and esteem in the eyes of others. God says, "A man who bears false witness against his neighbor is like a club, a sword, and a sharp arrow" (Proverbs 25:18). Indeed, God views character assassination as a form of murder! One of the things the Almighty lists in His holy Word as something He really hates is "a false witness who speaks lies."

(Proverbs 6:19). Deliberately spreading false rumors about someone or lying about him in formal testimony is a heinous violation of the law of God. False witnesses were employed at the blasphemy "trial" of Jesus Christ! "For many bore false witness against Him, but their testimonies did not agree" (Mark 14:56). God wants us to always speak the truth. "He who speaks truth declares righteousness, but a false witness, deceit. The truthful lip shall be established forever, but a lying tongue is but for a moment. Lying lips are an abomination to the LORD, but those who deal truthfully are His delight" (Proverbs 12:17, 19, 22). This doesn't mean, however, that we must always tell everything we know to those who seek to hurt others. The next verse says, "A prudent man conceals knowledge, but the heart of fools proclaims foolishness." We can be careful in how we present information. What we say must be the truth! It is only in seeking and bearing witness to the truth that a man can be associated with God - for God is Truth! The Bible calls Him the "God of truth" (Deu.32:4).

Jesus Christ, who is also God, proclaimed, "I am the way, the truth, and the life" (John 14:6). King David of ancient Israel wrote in praise to God, "Your law is truth. The entirety of your word is truth" (Ps. 119:142,151,160). Jesus Christ also prayed to the Father, "Your word is truth" (John17:17). Yes, everything that proceeds from the mouth of God is absolute Truth. "God is not a man, that He should lie" (Numbers 23:19). In the New Testament, we are told that "God cannot lie" (Titus 1:2) and "It is impossible for God to lie" (Hebrews 6:18).

Therefore, it is essential to approach God in truth. David explained, "The LORD is near to all who call upon Him, to all who call upon Him in truth" (Ps.145:18). And Jesus said, "God is Spirit, and those who worship Him must worship in spirit and truth" (John 4:24). If one's worship of God is not in Truth, then that person is not really worshipping Him. Anyone who lives by lies and deception will be rejected by the highest God. One must live by the truth! No matter what other personal weaknesses a human being may have, if he is willing to speak the truth, live openly and honestly, and acknowledge the truth when it is presented to him, he can be respected and helped to overcome his faults.

Even though honest differences of opinion permeate human society, everyone must learn to live and speak truthfully. Church services should make a difference to those who attend - if that church is truly Christian. Why? Because, as the Apostle John clearly says, genuinely Christian churchgoers are to be "walking in truth, as we received commandment from the Father" (2 John 4).

According to the Old Testament, "A false witness will not go unpunished, and he who speaks lies shall perish" (Proverbs 19:9). Perish? We've already seen that, in some ways, God equates the bearing of false witness with murder. Would He proclaim the same sentence for it? Just how seriously does God view infractions of His ninth commandment?

Under the civil law code God gave ancient Israel, murder was punishable by death. Could such a penalty also have been imposed for lying? "If a false witness rises against any man to testify against him of wrongdoing, then both men in the controversy shall stand before the LORD, before the priests and the judges who serve in those days. And the judges shall make diligent inquiry, and indeed, if the witness is a false witness, who has testified falsely against his brother, then you shall do to him as he thought to have done to his brother; so, you shall put away the evil person from among you. And those who remain shall hear and fear, and hereafter they shall not again commit such evil among you. Your eye shall not pity: life shall be for life, eye for eye, tooth for tooth, hand for hand, foot for foot" (Deu. 19:16-21). In ancient Israel, if it was discovered that you falsely accused someone of a capital crime, you would be executed! The final punishment for all sin is death (Romans 6:23) and lying is no exception. Truth will ultimately prevail. In the wonderful World Ahead, "Jerusalem shall be called the City of Truth." (Zech. 8:3). Lying will not be tolerated there. "But there shall by no means enter it anything that defiles, or causes an abomination or a lie, but only those who are written in the Lamb's Book of Life" (Revelation 21:27). Who won't make it into the New Jerusalem? "outside are dogs and sorcerers and sexually immoral and murderers and idolaters, and whoever loves and practices a lie" (Rev. 22:15). Where will they go? «The cowardly, unbelieving, abominable, murderers, sexually immoral, sorcerers, idolaters, and all liars shall have their part in the lake which burns with fire and brimstone, which is the second death" (Revelation 21:8). It should be plain to see that lying is serious with God. Again, those who seek God must always speak the truth. Yet our society is simply filled with lies! Nationally, we could well say to God, "For our transgressions are multiplied before you and our sins testify against us. Justice is turned back, and righteousness stands afar off; for truth is fallen in the street, and equity cannot enter. So, truth fails" (Isa. 59:12-15). Too often today the world›s judicial systems render precious little justice for the average person. These institutions of justice might be better termed "injustice systems." The Bible outlines that "Everyone will deceive his neighbour and will not speak the truth.

They have taught their tongue to speak lies. Your habitation is in the midst of deceit; through deceit they refuse to know Me" (Jer. 9:2-6). What is the result of lying? Blindness! The world is blind to the real nature of God and the plan He is working out here below. Jesus told religious authorities, who could not tolerate His Truth, "You are of your father the devil, and the desires of your father you want to do. He was a murderer from the beginning, and does not stand in the truth, because there is no truth in him. When he speaks a lie, he speaks from his own resources, for he is a liar and the father of it" (John 8:44).

CONCLUSION

Vigorous attempts to protect local culture from the homogenizing effects of globalisation are often intertwined with questionable, motives, including economic protectionism and the political suppression of ideas. As the topic of culture can, almost by definition, encompass almost every human endeavor, it is often difficult to draw lines around what are legitimate cultural activities, worthy of special protective measures. Globalisation critic Jeremy Rifkin has suggested there may be a need to establish a 'World Cultural Organisation' to help represent diverse cultures and put cultural protection on an equal footing with the WTO (Rifkin, 2001).Indeed, a "global" attempt to protect local cultures from "globalisation" would be a somewhat ironic development. Increasingly, local activists are trying to learn how to harness new worldwide forces to cope with the impact of international trends that have cultural effects. The International Network for Cultural Diversity has made a similar argument for an institution to ensure that culture is be protected. Their campaigns include protecting cultures in the Southern Hemisphere and using international legal instruments to protect culture (INCD, 2003).

Broad trends such as the globalisation of 21st century technology, increased international and transnational industrial as well as economic activity have helped drive the globalisation. In response to the globalisation of the world, it is the task of public policy to minimize the risks and maximize the benefits to ensure the ongoing global innovation that is essential to the world's economy, global security. and the facilitation of continued access to the new knowledge generated by global network.Building a robust and effective global strategy for ensuring world access to the results of networks will also require obtaining a better understanding of current trends in global network worldwide. We mist define in a clear and focused manner the critical questions and challenges must address to meet global economic shifts. This includes considering defence, and global security needs; as well as developing a renewed approach to managing regulatory regimes, improving the education system, and strengthening the infrastructure for global network.

My wife and Children

My wife and Children

My wife and Children: Rev. Canon Elizabeth Nyandeng Kuol

Elijah Abuoi Arok

My sons, John Payai, David Kuir and Abraham Deng

BIBLIOGRAPHY

Andreatta Susan (Jan. 1 2012). Elements of Culture: An Applied Perspective Wadsworth Publishing; 1 edition.

Andregg M. Micheal. (January 1, 2014) Seven Billion and Counting: The Crisis in Global Population Growth Library Binding.

Baird Mark.(May 2013) An American Crisis: Veterans' Unemployment : Stand by Them/How You Can Help/Solutions: Caleb Publications.

Banks A. James. (Jan 21, 2018) An Introduction to Multicultural Education (What's New in Foundations / Intro to Teaching 6th Edition.

Banks A. James McGee Banks A. (December 4, 2015) Multicultural Education: Issues and Prespectives

Bearden M. David and Copeland Claudia. (December 21, 2013) Environmental Laws: Summaries of Major Statutes Administered by the Environmental Protection Agency

Budg M. Kathleen and Parret H. William. (January 25, 2018) Disrupting Poverty: Five Powerful Classroom Practices.

Cooper D. Terry. (July 5, 2003) Sin, Pride & Self-Acceptance: The Problem of Identity in Theology & Psychology.

Charan Ram. (February 2013) Global Tilt : Leading Your Business Through the Great Economic Power Shift: Crown Publishing Group

Channar Ali Zahid. (April 27, 2012) Gender Discrimination at Workplace.

Delisle R. James (January 16, 2018) Doing Poorly on Purpose: Strategies to Reverse Underachievement and Respect Student Dignity.

Dicken PeterJune.(6, 2003) Global Shift: Reshaping the Global Economic Map in the 21st Century 4th Edition

Dickson Peter. (February 10, 2015) Global Shift: Mapping the Changing Contours of the World Economy: The Guilford Press; 7th Edition

Falk Richard. (August, 2016) Power Shift: On the New Global Order.

Ferguson J Susan. (Nov.21, 2012) Mapping the Social Landscape: Readings in Sociology. McGraw-Hill Education; 7 editions.

Grabb Larry. (June 17, 2014) Fully Alive: A Biblical Vision of Gender That Frees Men and Women to Live Beyond Stereotypes.

Grover Tricia.(October 1, 2017) Walk It Out: The Radical Result of Living God's Word One Step at a Time.

Guis Stephen. (November 27, 2016) Mini Habits for Weight Loss: Stop Dieting. Form New Habits. Change Your Lifestyle Without Suffering. Kindle Edition

Gurung Uday. (October 14, 2010) Caste Discrimination and Poverty: a Case Study of Dalit Women in Nepal.

Grusec E. Joan &Hastings D. Paul. (Nov. 25, 2015). Handbook of Socialization: Theory and Research: The Guilford Press; 2 edition

Havens Jeff. (April 2010) How to Get Fired!: The New Employee's Guide to Perpetual Unemployment.

Hughes Phil and Ferrett Ed. (November 2, 2015) Introduction to Health and Safety at Work: for the NEBOSH National General Certificate in Occupational Health and Safety 6th Edition

Jackson Yvett. (March 25, 2011) The Pedagogy of Confidence: Inspiring High Intellectual Performance in Urban Schools.

Jensen Eric. (November 19, 2009) Teaching With Poverty In Mind: What Being Poor Does to Kids' Brains and What Schools Can Do About It 1st Edition

Karade Jaga. (August 1, 2015) Caste Discrimination.

Keane David. (September 28, 2007) Caste-based Discrimination in International Human Rights Law 1st Edition.

Keidar Michal and Yuval Nurit.(August 27, 2015) Children book: One, Two, Family: A single parent family.

Kikel Charlotte. (January 9, 2018) Eat in Peace to Live in Peace: Your Handbook for Vitality Kindle Edition

Killermann Sam. (September 4, 2013) The Social Justice Advocate's Handbook: A Guide to Gender

Knox L.Paul and McCarthy M. Linda (November 14, 2011) Urbanization: An Introduction to Urban Geography.

Lanman A. Barry and Wendling M. Laura (November 7, 2013). Preparing the Next Generation of Oral Historians: An Anthology of Oral History Education

Lipman Pauline. (January 15, 2004) High Stakes Education: Inequality, Globalization, and Urban School Reform (Critical Social Thought).

Macionis J. John. (January 12, 2014) Society: The Basics 13th Edition.

McCarney T. Kevin. (September 1, 2011). The Secrets of Successful Communication: A Simple

Mettler Suzanne. (March 11, 2016) Degrees of Inequality: How the Politice of Higher Education Sabotage the American Dream

Mullen L. Ann. (December 12, 2011 Degrees of Inequality: Culture, Class, and Gender in American Higher Education

Newton E. David.(January 15, 2016) Overpopulation: 7 Billion People and Counting (The End of Life As We Know It) Library Binding.

Park L. Robert. (July 21, 2010) Superstition: Belief in the Age of Science 1st Edition.

Parret H. William and Budg M. Kathleen. (January 5, 2012) Turning High-Poverty Schools into High-Performing Schools.

Patterson Kerry. (Sep. 9, 2011). Crucial Conversations Tools for Talking When Stakes Are High: McGraw-Hill Education; 2 editions.

Sanford L. Mark and Wilkens Steve. (October 22, 2009) Hidden

Worldviews: Eight Cultural Stories That Shape Our Lives.

Sax Leonard. (August 29, 2017) Why Gender Matters: What Parents and Teachers Need to Know About the Emerging Science of Sex Differences Second Edition.

Schuette L. (February 1, 2010. Sarah Single-Parent Families (My Family).

Schuckit A. Marc. (December 18, 2003 Drug and Alcohol Abuse: A Clinical Guide to Diagnosis and Treatment 6th Edition.

Smyles Iris.(June 2016) Dating Tips for the Unemployed.

Tuner E. Marlene. (Sept.3, 2000). Groups at Work: Theory and Research (Applied Social Research Series): Psychology Press 0th Edition

Weisman Alan.(May 6, 2014) Countdown: Our Last, Best Hope for a Future on Earth?

Wytsma Ken.(May 14, 2017) The Myth of Equality: Uncovering the Roots of Injustice/ Privilege

tent.com/pod-product-compliance
e LLC
PA
)10526
)053B/1766